RACHA

The Ten Commandments
of
#SuccessWithoutApology

outskirts
press

Dedicated to my WystleDolls, past, present, and future

Thank you for allowing me to be a part of your journey of success.

#Wystledolls4life

#IntegrityWorksHere

TABLE OF CONTENTS

PREFACE

Whistles blowing, sneakers screeching, and coaches and parents yelling, that is the sound of the summer weekend basketball camp in Baltimore, where I first encounter Missy. She and I are NCAA Division I Women's basketball referees; we are both trying out for a spot on the A10 officiating staff. A short lunch ride to Applebees, I conclude Missy is one of the funniest women I know. I like her. She's quick witted, but I'm noticing a pause after each laugh as her mind drifts to someplace a million miles away. Her humorous "gameface" may fool everyone else, but I see her sadness as a reflection of my own. Weeks of friendship pass before she confides in me, but eventually she confirms what I had suspected. Publicly, she is a strong woman. Privately, she is battling the daily requirement to apologize for her ambition, passion, strength, and success. She, like so many of us, thrives at work, apologizes at home, and then feels guilt about both. When I met Missy, I met someone I recognized from my personal mirror.

Our friendship over the next few years became foundational for the person I am today. We traveled, talked on the phone daily, recommended encouraging books, and survived our heartbreaks together. We developed a bond of friendship I further describe in chapters seven and eight, but know she was an essential companion who helped me really "see" myself and encouraged me to find my new best self that would have the courage to write this book.

Along our journey of recovery, Missy and I chose to read Tommy Newberry's book, *40 Days to a Joy-Filled Life*. Inspired by Newberry's book and the way in which he leaves the reader with a takeaway at the end of each chapter, I have formatted mine in much the same way. I encourage you to record your thoughts in the box-outs, to reflect in the blank pages, and to identify personal and professional situations in which you can practice each commandment. Ultimately, I want you to claim and attain success your way. I will arm you with ten commandments for achieving your #SuccessWithoutApology.

In future chapters I'll ask you to challenge society--including your own family and friends if necessary--to accept your success without expecting an apology from you. Your personal views and your relationships may evolve as a result of your new perspective. This is good; it's good for your growth and for your journey of self-discovery. So don't panic. Face your own challenges. Accept that you are different. You desire success and greatness in a new way. It's time to build a world where your desire isn't shoved aside. For the sake of your employees, your children, and for women around the world, together, we must change society's view and acceptance of the modern successful women.

As you read these commandments and plan to attend one of my speaking events, I passionately encourage you to become the greatest version of yourself. Earn as much money as you can, run your longest race, live a lifestyle free of guilt, be a great parent and partner, and enjoy your successes with the person/people you love. This is my charge to you, and I hold you personally responsible. The only person who can keep you from becoming the best version of yourself is you. *The Ten Commandments of #SuccessWithoutApology* is about freeing your mind to enjoy the ride, it's about uncovering your excuses, releasing your unnecessary guilt, and overcoming the fear of other people's perceptions so that you can in fact realize your best self.

So where do you begin?

"The hard part is putting one word after another." Jo Linsdell
If beginning is half the battle, finishing is the other half, right? To finish a book, you have to just keep putting one word right after another until the end. Then possibly rewrite those words a few dozen times until you are satisfied. While in the thick of rewrites, discouraged about whether I would ever complete it, people often asked what the book was going to be about. I always have a very good elevator speech (small business lesson #1 – always have an elevator speech handy). But it is important that you, the reader, understand why I wrote this book for you personally. I believe society wants women to succeed. It really does rah rah for our success. Unfortunately, as we achieve glimpses of such desired success, we – especially women – are having a hard time figuring out what that means for the rest of our private life, family life, friendships, and traditional roles and responsibilities. We are stuck in the place of trying to meet the demands of our new-found, hard-fought success while achieving our preconceived ideas of the perfect wife, mom, daughter, friend, etc. We're simply trying to do it all – and it is IMPOSSIBLE.

We apologize to people around us all day, feeling incompetent. That is ridiculous and holding us back. So I want to clearly state my intentions and purpose of *The Ten Commandments of #SuccessWithoutApology*. The book's three distinct objectives are:

> **Elevator Pitch**: A slang term used to describe a brief speech that outlines an idea for a product, service or project. The name comes from the notion that the speech should be delivered in the short time period of an elevator ride, usually 20-60 seconds

1. Encourage women who want to build a career, a family, and a legacy

2. Improve the world's viewpoint of successful women

3. Expand my influence through mentorship and legacy building

The first two objectives are directed towards you and all humankind, but the third one is personal. You might raise your eyebrows at point number three, but I do not apologize for having one objective about my success and my goals. This attitude of ownership you'll learn to embrace throughout the following chapters and commandments. Writing and publishing this book is a step on my success ladder and as you read it, you are a part of my success too. #sorrynotsorry #EnjoyTheJourney

When you picked up this book, what attracted you to it? Why did you think you needed to read it? Do you expect to glean anything in particular from my ten commandments? Do you have a purpose for reading this book? Is your purpose for yourself or for other women you know? Let's establish and note your purpose for reading *Ten Commandments of #SuccessWithoutApology*. We'll check back at the end of the book to see if you found what you were looking for in here.

What is your purpose for reading this book?

_____

_____

_____

_____

_____

TAKE CREDIT

Studies have shown that women put others' needs ahead of their own, and we often give others the credit for our successes. A May 2013 study published in the "Personality and Social Psychology Bulletin" found that women who work with men are far less likely to take credit for their work than those who collaborate with other women. Why is that? And what do we need to do to stop that from happening? We must first give ourselves permission to take the credit.

We can have success, and we can own it with pride. Here is a scenario, with two different responses, I have unfortunately witnessed numerous times: The male executive receives praise in the board room for a great advertising campaign that he pitched to a client. He responds with something to the effect of, "Thank you. I identified the decision maker and ensured we addressed her greatest concerns. Once she bought in, I was able to receive consensus and move forward with my suggestion. The client loved me."

Same scenario: A female executive receives praise in the board room for a great advertising campaign she pitched to a client and her response is something like, "Thank you. It was the combined effort of a great team. Everyone went the extra mile to hit the deadlines and present a great presentation of what our overall team can do. I couldn't have done it without a full team effort. I was simply leading a dedicated group with great talent."

Sound familiar? Ladies, STOP IT! Stop sharing the glory when you rocked your role. You managed the direction. You led the strategy. You were great. Take the credit when the credit is due. Which leads me to state my mission in this phase of life: to support, encourage, and challenge women of all ages to own their path to success, especially if the route is non-traditional. Though I own a boutique gift shop in Oklahoma, named Wystle (pronounced whistle), I know that the ownership of a brick and mortar business will not be my legacy. Within those walls, I am daily building a legacy of personal and business mentoring relationships. I don't leave my legacy to chance, hoping I impact those around me. Rather, I state my desire to be a mentor and my willingness to be my mentee's greatest cheerleader for success. I am called to train, teach, and inspire the people who enter my shop and my life. Whether they come in to have their hair done by one of my stylists, or to punch a time clock for a paycheck, they are important to my life's work. The way in which I hopefully impact their lives will be my legacy. Do you know what you want your legacy to be? Do you know what your success will mean for others? If so, what are you doing each day to write your story, to build your legacy?

People tell me I have achieved success somewhat unconventionally.

I've experienced a highly unique combination of jobs and experiences. So yes, I am a little different, and yes, I am good with that. The fact that I am an NCAA Women's basketball referee is probably a good clue to the fact that, I "ain't like most women you know." #SuccessMyWay #SorryNotSorry

GIVE CREDIT

As I have advanced throughout my career, I have been super fortunate to have incredibly supportive, confident, and intelligent men and women mentors. They did not expect me to fit the mold of the traditional female executive. They encouraged me to express my emotions, use my woman's intuition, and balance my personal and professional life. Early in my officiating career and my corporate career, I was watching every move of the successful women in the workplace. I noticed they were expected to act like men, to respond like men, and to keep everything that was personal suppressed lest they be seen as weak, vulnerable, or out of balance. What a crock! I saw no sign of me succeeding if I had to play by those rules.

Women have so much to offer, why expect us to act like something we are not? Let's use our God-given talents. We are great multi-taskers and delegators. We balance high-level professional jobs while maintaining a household, sparingly sharing the workload. We drive carpools. We cook. We clean. We love. We care. We volunteer. We still experience the guilt of not doing enough. We feel guilt about not parenting as well as our own parents. We carry guilt about not

---

What are you doing each day to establish your legacy?

_____

_____

_____

_____

_____

_____

_____

_____

_____

_____

_____

_____

"wife-ing" as well as our own mother, guilt about not making anything from Pinterest. We have guilt about not perfectly balancing our life like other women seem to do. We spend so much of our day apologizing for not meeting unreasonable expectations. #DamnGuilt #DamnPinterest #WhoSetTheseStandards

The reality is, our success does not look the same as it did for our grandmothers. It is incumbent on each of us to quit feeling guilty when we work 40+ hours a week, order takeout, hire a house cleaner, and forget to bake anything for the church potluck. We should stop feeling guilty for not doing the same thing as the generations before us. We are doing life and success differently and we must begin setting our own terms.

If I have struck a nerve, if I have described your guilt, then you are prime for living *The Ten Commandments of #SuccessWithoutApology*. In this book, I will give you personal stories of success and failure. I will explore traits of modern day, successful women. I will assure you, for the glass ceiling to be broken, women must consciously stop apologizing for exhibiting the normal behaviors of successful people. We must own our own success. And we must begin removing all of the "I am sorry's" from our daily dialogue.

I have written this book to help you display the confidence to succeed without apology. If you occasionally catch yourself apologizing, as even I do, don't give up. Don't stop making an effort to change. When you notice how much people (usually women) apologize, you will want to share this book. Let's change our culture by apologizing less and by learning to accept our own successes, because we earned it!

In the following chapters, I will expand upon each of the following Ten Commandments of #SuccessWithoutApology. Feel free to take your time reading through these commandments and to share your own story on my blog, www.successwithoutapology.com. This book is the beginning of a conversation between my readers and friends from around the globe and myself.

Here are my ten commandments for success without apology:

1. **Do not apologize for wanting success (being focused and driven).**
2. **Do not apologize for your motherhood status.**
3. **Do not apologize for working late.**
4. **Do not apologize when you pivot.**
5. **Do not apologize for taking care of yourself.**
6. **Do not apologize for emotions (yours or others).**
7. **Do not apologize for friendships and loyalty.**
8. **Do not apologize for supporting other women.**
9. **Do not apologize for being the boss.**
10. **Do not apologize for reaping the rewards of success.**

Have you ever left a meeting or conference with pages full of notes, yet felt completely overwhelmed? I imagine Moses may have felt the same way when he came off the mountaintop with the Lord's Ten Commandments written on the front and back of two heavy pieces of stone.

The Ten Commandments of #SuccessWithoutApology, I can assure you, are much easier to carry than the stone tablets Moses carried down from the mountain. But it is going to take an army of us carrying them to change our culture. I see women like Reese Witherspoon affecting Hollywood with female leading roles, and Tyra Banks creating jobs for women to have a little "F.U. money," and Hillary Clinton running for President of the United States of America, and I see women inspiring women. I see culture slowly changing, but it is too slow. We must do more. Our culture is not evolving fast enough for women. According to *The Institute of Women's Policy* Research, women's earning power today in the United States:

> "They are the equal, if not the main, breadwinner in four out of ten families. They receive more college and graduate degrees than men. Yet, on average, women continue to earn considerably less than men. In 2015, female full-time workers made only 79 cents for every dollar earned by men, a gender wage gap of 21 percent." #Unfreakinbelievable

That does not fly in our house. My husband loves to tell you how hard I work. He never asks me to apologize for earning more or working more. Yet he is so discouraged and frustrated when men earn more than me while doing the same or less work. I have been living the life of an entrepreneur for two decades, all while holding a full-time corporate job. I began writing this book because I was ashamed of the bosses who wanted me to apologize for achieving and enjoying success differently than them. I began writing because I was proud of my success. Yet, these men wanted to pay me less because I didn't live where they lived or join the clubs they joined. They penalized me for asking why there were no women executives in their club. I was representative of statistics reported by the *Bureau of Labor Statistics Weekly News Release* dated July 19, 2016:

- Median weekly earnings of full-time workers were $824 in the second quarter of 2016. Women had median weekly earnings of $744, or 81.8 percent of the $909 median for men.

- The women's-to-men's earnings ratio varied by race and ethnicity. White women earned 80.7 percent as much as their male counterparts, compared with Black women (91.8 percent), Asian women (79.1 percent), and Hispanic women (89.1 percent)

Men earned more than me because they were men – not because of experience or expertise. #ThatsBullShit

In these pages, I will share what I have observed in both successful men and women over the course of my career, what I have learned through failure, and what I believe we must do to help women earn equal pay, equal respect, and equal job titles. If you are ready to push women's personal and professional success to another level, then you are ready to stop apologizing.

Before we begin with the first commandment...

Tell me what you last apologized for unnecessarily.

_____

_____

_____

Tell me what success means for you right now.

_____

_____

_____

_____

I figure if a girl wants to become a legend,
she should just go ahead and be one.

Martha Jane (Calamity Jane) Cannary 1852-1903

Chapter One
WANTING SUCCESS

First Commandment: Do not apologize for wanting success.
2. Do not apologize for your motherhood status.
3. Do not apologize for working late.
4. Do not apologize when you pivot.
5. Do not apologize for taking care of yourself.
6. Do not apologize for emotions (yours or others).
7. Do not apologize for friendships and loyalty.
8. Do not apologize for supporting other women.
9. Do not apologize for being the boss.
10. Do not apologize for reaping the rewards of success.

I know it may seem in bad taste to site the Bible in the introduction and Calamity Jane in the next chapter, but hey, I truly believe that inspiration can come from anywhere. This contradiction is symbolic of my experiences, ranging from my very religious and traditional upbringing, to a corporate world that would have seemed like the Wild West for a little Oklahoma country girl! For anyone too young to know of Calamity Jane, she was a notorious character, dissolute and devilish, but self-supportive and successful in her own rite. Legend has it, she held jobs as a dishwasher, cook, waitress, dance-hall girl, nurse, and even, when necessary, the occasional stints of prostitution. But then again, half of her stories may not even be true, as she was quite the famed spinner of yarns--#sorrynotsorry may have been her life motto.

She interests me because she *decided* to be a legend, and she told her story the way *she* wanted it told. Now, in 2017 we still only know mostly what *she* wanted us to know about her life. She's still exerting influence over her legacy even one hundred years later! Calamity Jane's quote, used to introduce this chapter, puts the onus on us girls. If we want success, we must go get it. If we want to become a legend, we are responsible for writing our story. This is the mentality that I want to inspire in you. If you want it, go get it.

Leading into this chapter, you stated what success meant to you, and now I give you the freedom to chase that success without apology. Determine what it takes to reach those personal and professional wants/goals. Consider how you will prepare the people around you to support your success rather than resist it or fight it. If you desire success for yourself then that will become part of your legacy. You will have a legacy, one way or the other. Why not, in the spirit of Calamity Jane, write your own...

How will you be remembered? Begin now, declaring your legacy.

People will say you were:

_____

_____

_____

_____

_____

You will be remembered for doing:

_____

_____

_____

_____

In the spirit of the Wild Wild West, let me introduce you to my two young cowboy nephews, Cutter and Cactus, and my athletic nieces, Alexis and Payton. My nephews and nieces are very talented kids with supportive, successful, hard working, country-living parents.

Cutter, who is not yet a teenager, wakes up each morning and ropes the dummy 100 times before he goes to school. (A dummy is a mechanical version of a steer, allowing cowboys to practice roping without all the preparation of saddling horses and corralling cattle.) He practices his roping skills daily because he wants to win every roping, every time. (He is ten, and not competitive at all—ha.) I have heard people ask him about this habit, and their reaction is almost always one of admiration for his devotion and drive. On the other hand, I witness very different reactions to my sixteen-year-old niece, who spends her Saturdays, Sundays, and most school day afternoons practicing basketball. While she may not be the fastest or the tallest, she works hard. Because of her drive and determination she has shown significant improvement year after year. Yet, when she tells people (including some of my own family) about her commitment to being the best basketball player possible, they don't respond to her the same positive way as they do to my nephew. They shrug at her athletic ambitions, and wonder why she doesn't care more about her social life, church activities and boys. Cutter's focus and determination is viewed differently than Payton's, though both are showing similar drive and discipline towards success. The bias is a cultural standard based upon their gender. I believe people's comments, words, and perceptions that make up this double standard are not intentional – but indicative of a deeply-ingrained societal prejudice.

I have seen it multiple times and even experienced it during my own competitive sport days. I don't believe that people are even necessarily cognizant of their varying reactions to boys versus girls. When my niece responds to a question with, "No, I can't because I have basketball practice," many react with a trite expression such as, "There's more to life than basketball." While this sort of prejudice is subtle, it is still hugely impactful. That simple statement can detour a young girl's focus and drive. Fortunately, my niece is more confident at 16 than I was, and she is okay with their responses. #SheWillSucceedDespiteThem #ThatDontMakeItRight

So how can we empower young women and consequently encourage and cheer on their drive and devotion? You may look at me now and think I was always driven and unapologetic, but I wasn't. It has been a long, hard-fought journey, one that may have cost me a marriage along the way. And though my ex-husband didn't support my dreams and desires, I was fortunate enough to have a few business mentors in my life who did! Warren, Tony, and Carr would never want the spotlight of appreciation and gratitude, but I would be remiss if I didn't mention and thank them.

In my last full-time job for Tony and Carr (co-owners), I commuted to New York City every other week. I was the Vice President of Sales & New Business for their Maryland based company, but most of my advertising clients were located in the Big Apple. Why would a Maryland / New York City company hire someone from Oklahoma to be a sales exec? I will name three reasons.

#1: I am driven.

#2: I build lasting and meaningful relationships.

#3: I can sell ice to Eskimos! (Seriously, #GirlCanSell)

But even so, how does a graduate of a small private school like Oklahoma Baptist University end up working for two Ivy League attorneys in a fast-paced New York City company? Well, there is a story...

#TrueStory: I was working for a real estate tycoon, Warren, and managing his historical properties in Shawnee, Oklahoma. One of the buildings had a tenant that published a magazine called, *The CPA Technology Advisor*. While working for Warren, I was going to school to earn a Property Management Certification, and I took the lead in several lease negotiations and renewals. Particularly, I worked on some very complicated lease agreements with a media company, negotiating opposite a very savvy woman who happened to be the publisher of this magazine.

One day she asked to meet. Honestly, I expected her to complain about the heating and air conditioning again. #StrugglesInHistoricProperties However, she surprised me with the announcement of her recent promotion, and an offer to interview as the next publisher. I distinctly remember asking her, "What does a publisher do?" (Not that I am suggesting you should EVER ask this question in an interview, just sayin'.) But the way she answered the question had a significant impact on me, and I've used the line many times since. She said, "Don't worry about what you are selling because I can teach you the products on the shelf. You are smart, confident, and you know how to build and maintain relationships, and that I cannot teach. The products and services you will learn." Looking back, during all those hours of negotiating leases and maintaining proper air conditioning for the client, I was actually preparing for my big break. And here I thought I was just learning about HVAC, historical preservation rules, and basement tiles. But, it turns out, I was making an impact on my future supervisor, boss, and (now) great friend. #NeverMissAnOpportunity #EveryoneIsSomeone #HVAC2NYC

At that time, a publisher's role had not been on my radar. Growth, opportunity, and money, however, were very much on my radar! When the opportunity presented itself, I evaluated it against the three items of my new-job-litmus-test. I tell women I mentor that each job you accept should offer a significant increase in at least one of the following three areas:

1. Title and responsibility
2. Network and opportunity
3. Pay

Receiving more than one is an added bonus, but don't change jobs unless you get at least one of the three. In the case of the publishing opportunity, I made the decision based on the pay. But it was the networking opportunities that became my greatest reward from the role. When offered the position, I was six years into my marriage, and I had already forgiven my husband for his first alleged affair. I was fragile to say the least. Because of my personal doubts, this opportunity became more than a job. It symbolized financial independence in the event that my husband should leave me. My inner insecurity drove my outward confidence, and soon, I became the most profitable, bottom-line boosting publisher within the organization. I am forever grateful to that smart lady who hand-picked me to be her successor. #ThanksShari

While it may not be on your radar today, would you consider a new job? If so, which of these three benefits would you seek or want the most?

> **Would you leave your job for title and responsibility, network and opportunity, or pay?**
>
> _____
> _____
> _____
> _____
> _____
>
> **Why?**
>
> _____
> _____
> _____

Annually as publishers, we prepared and presented the upcoming year's projections, budgets, and business plan to the CEO, CFO, CTO, and a handful of other executives. Being the only woman in the room, this situation was intimidating, especially to a twenty-something female. But I did my homework, studied the industry along with my competition, and dedicated nights and weekends to being the smartest, most informed publisher in the company.

During presentation week in Fort Atkinson, Wisconsin, I met the co-CEO's of Cygnus Business Media, Tony and Carr. My drive and salesmanship made an impression on them, and years later they told me that my confidence and understanding of my market really helped them to believe in my business plan. Soon after I left Cygnus Business Media's 500+ employee organization, I rejoined Tony and Carr at one of their startup companies. This amazing new role checked the networking and responsibility boxes for me, and I began engaging with the most prestigious advertising executives in digital media, from the likes of the late Ari Bluman, to Dave Moore, to Nicolle Pangis, to David Bell, and to Brian Gleason. I credit Tony and Carr for looking past a southern accent and an Oklahoma mailing address to see a professional who could sell and grow a business for them. They were the first professionals to invite me (the girl) to play golf, smoke a cigar, and lean-in to the decision-making process of a very complex and fast-paced technology business. #ForeverGrateful #CountryGirl4Life #GirlsCanRunBusinesses2

Because of them, I made a lot of money. I loved working for these guys, and I really did consider it a dream job. But when they sold the business, and I worked for the new ownership for a year, WOW did I miss them more than ever. Instead of my dream job, with both professional and personal support and trust, I was now working for a closed-minded, male chauvinist, elitist CEO. The new CEO fostered a handcuffed and distrustful working environment for me, as well as for any other woman recognized as an industry expert. No amount of drive, confidence, or desire was going to help me advance (which he told me so - point blank). The year I spent laboring to prove a woman could make decisions, that a remote employee could be an efficient employee, and that women should have a voice in the boardroom, was the worst year of my adult life. #SexismStillExists

The contrast in the two male-led working environments, and my new realization of male chauvinism in the workplace, spurred my desire to write and speak up about a culture in need of a major overhaul. And after spending a year mentoring a woman in Tunisia through the George W. Bush *Women's Initiative Fellowship*, I better understood the need for change beyond the United States. I want to affect society, not just in America, but globally. Hey go big or go home right…I want to make the closed-minded male CEO a thing of the past. To do so, I need women **and men** to make this change in their family and their workplace. Be a change agent like Warren, Tony, and Carr – not a hater like my last CEO, who shall remain nameless as he's simply not worth the energy it would take to type his name. #HatersGonnaHate

Before selling the company, Tony and Carr encouraged my professional growth and provided me with the freedom to pursue my personal goals outside the organization. While working for them, I was simultaneously advancing my career as an NCAA Division I

Women's basketball referee, which consisted of refereeing basketball games all over the country from November through March. I was burning the candle at both ends and loving every minute of it. When other people were leaving work to go to a child's lacrosse game or to prepare dinner for their spouse, I was catching a flight to referee a game in another time zone. Being supported and encouraged to pursue my passions made me a better employee — it gave me the energy and fire to be the best salesperson in the company. I worked on planes, in between games, in hotels, whatever I had to do. An added bonus: sometimes I officiated basketball games in the same cities as existing clients, and I could drop in and build relationships while I was in town. #AlwaysBuildingRelationships #AlwaysBeClosing #SuccessIsntConfined2ACubicle

I love being the sales person, and I love being the referee, so I did both. I do both. After working for people who "get it," I quickly learned to recognize employers who did not understand how the competitiveness of officiating actually made me a better employee. I steer clear of those employers now. Often, they are the same employers who think women with children are subsequently too distracted to give the company their best. Yet another highly charged subject when it comes to women in the workplace. (See next commandment) #IgnoranceByChoice

To those people who discriminate against mothers, I ask: have you ever noticed how women with three children run a household? They can multitask and problem-solve as well as any employee - I promise you that. #AintThatRightLindsay And to those mothers who are scared to go back to work or afraid to mention your children in an interview — stop apologizing. Embrace your strengths. Embrace your experience as the Chief Operations Officer-Head Chef-Project Manager-Driver-Mother. Your skillset outside of the office is what many businesses need, and you can always take a class for the PowerPoint skills. You know what they can not teach you. Do not apologize for wanting success, a family, and respect.

The choice to not have children is selfish. Life rejuvenates and acquires energy when it multiplies: It is enriched, not impoverished.

Pope Francis, 2015

Chapter Two
MOTHERHOOD STATUS

1. Do not apologize for wanting success.

Second Commandment: Do not apologize for your motherhood status.

3. Do not apologize for working late.
4. Do not apologize when you pivot.
5. Do Not Apologize for Taking Care of Yourself.
6. Do not apologize for emotions (yours or others).
7. Do not apologize for friendships and loyalty.
8. Do not apologize for outsourcing.
9. Do not apologize for being the boss.
10. Do not apologize for reaping the rewards of success.

I ended the last chapter highlighting the strengths of mothers, and I believe that women who have children have been particulary discriminated against in the workforce. I want to thank all the working moms who have sacrificed and paved the way for today's moms. You made huge sacrifices while standing up to the good ol' boy culture that pervades many organizations. I applaud mothers who have started their own businesses, entered the armed forces, and/or succeeded in the corporate world. You are all rock stars in my book. (Insert applause here.) #ThanksMom

But to be clear: women have the right to have children or not have children. Women also have the right to work or not work. But parental success doesn't have to be instead of and in place of business success. Women can do both, and they can make the rules in terms of what works best for their family. We all know those celebrity moms who manage to make it look easy, who have high-powered careers and wonderful families. Women like: Faith Hill, Indra Nooyi (chairman and chief of PepsiCo), Jada Pinkett Smith or Ivanka Trump. I personally know plenty of women who do success in their own way, who are successful at work and raise children on their own terms. Some of my role models, my friends - Audrey, Kelli, Leigh-Anne, Erika and Lolly (to name a few). They define their own success, different of course from that of their moms. They are setting examples for young women and men, and they are daily breaking societal molds. (Insert applause here)

These women are uniquely remarkable. Some, like Kelli, work in a super high-stress role, equally or even more demanding than her husband's career. She tries all the latest order-in conveniences like meal delivery and house cleaning, all so she can spend her time at home engaged in quality activities, like school crafts or pool parties. She is a rock star. Then there's my friend Leigh-Anne who worked her way up the corporate ladder of pharmaceutical sales to negotiate a job share program where she works one week on, followed by one week off. This arrangement allows her to be a classroom mom, a stay-at-home professional mom who earns and fights half the month, but can still tell corporate America to piss off the other half of the month. She's another brave rock star, breaking the mold for other women to follow suit.

All of these ladies parent and work, and they redefine the norm. They're cool with fighting this fight—which I love. They do it for the great example this struggle sets for their children. They do it because it works for their family. And because of this, they are my heroes. #Mompreneur #MomsRule

As brave as these women are, most still haven't quite figured out how to label this new and seemingly unconventional image of MOM. They still battle their own personal versions of feeling inadequate. Women continue to have bosses who think they will be too distracted or won't be able to keep the long hours if they are parents or work from home. I'd like to think we've progressed since my interview, nearly 20 years ago now, when the man quizzed me in multiple ways about whether or not I was planning to have children. It was not out of concern for me as a human, but out of fear his company would suffer if I became a young mom. I hope we have made progress, but sometimes I hear stories that make me fear we have not. #TrueStory #YouCantAskMeThatCanYou

If you enter an interview or role where you think you may face this same opposition, can you articulate your amazing mom skills as business skills? Do not apologize for being a woman who also has life experience running a home, a carpool, and a PTA. Right now – claim your skills- claim those skills and write them as though they were interview skills.

Name skills you use outside the office that make you a great employee and/or boss.

_____

_____

_____

SKILLS IN ACTION

All women are not alike, just as all families are not. My family was definitely outside the "norm" for many of you reading this book. I was the second of four children. My mother started working out of the home when I was five years old. By the time I was in junior high, she was working on a full-time basis, running two small companies. And when I left for college, she was the primary breadwinner of our family. I remember men did not take her seriously as a woman business owner. I remember the prejudice she received and the chauvinism she endured when she ran her first business out of an old armory building.

My mom may be humble, but she doesn't back down easily. She is accommodating, but firm when it comes to her principles. I know certain people disrespected her, or whispered about her for working so hard while raising us. But my mom was and is a rock star. She was raised by a God-fearing man who told her she could be anything she wanted to be, and he taught her to use the tools in his main street hardware store so she could be self-sufficient too if she wanted. So without apology, she did just that.

My mother wasn't one to apologize for her drive, though she may have had insecurities along the way. My dad, exemplary like her Father, supported her at every turn. He was a true partner to my mom, and he never told her she couldn't raise her children, start her own businesses, *and* be Volunteer of the Year. He quietly and simply supported her— he was her unseen foundation. He was a tough, rugged cowboy with nothing but pride in his outgoing, strong, businesswoman bride. Now that's a man!

You can find all sorts of books, blogs, and motivational series on the topic of balancing motherhood and business. And again, my mom may be the perfect living embodiment of this balance. But what about those women who have all the same desires for family, and for becoming the perfect wife, but don't have children? I am one of those women. I am a family woman; I love my husband dearly and will put my family above all else, but I never felt called to birth children. I do have a wonderful stepdaughter, who has been more like a girlfriend since she came into my life when she was 19 years old. She is the greatest woman in my husband's life, and his love for her is beyond words. And yes, I've heard, it is a love I will never know. I am that woman – the one who will never REALLY understand a mother's love. I am the barren woman. The one who is now more common than ever in the workforce, and yet still not fully accepted from a societal, social and overall 'mainstream' American perspective. We, the barren, are questioned and are often defending our choice. #TheyStopAskingAfter40 #AlmostAgedOut

The truth is, many people including Pope Francis, feel a woman's choice to not have children is profoundly selfish. The quote with which I opened this chapter was from Pope Francis in 2015: "The choice to not have children is selfish. Life rejuvenates and acquires energy when it multiplies: It is enriched, not impoverished." Pope Francis is considered one of the most beloved popes in history, and his acceptance of different people has been unprecedented in the Catholic church, yet he scorns women like me and calls us selfish for not birthing children. *Time* magazine even named him Person of the Year and lauded him with language like, "What makes this Pope so important is the speed with which he has captured the imaginations of millions who had given up on hoping for the church at all."[3]

To be clear, I love kids. I do. I love to babysit, teach and interact with children of all ages. Yet, I have always known I was not going to have children of my own. Some may say God revealed this to me in my early teens, others will say I have always been too busy or, a la Pope Francis, am too selfish. You can choose your opinion, just know, I won't apologize for my choice. #SorryNotSorry

My first experience of direct backlash because of this decision was when it cost me my high school sweetheart. We had been dating about 6 months before I left for Australia as an exchange student. Upon returning, I spent an evening with him that significantly changed the direction of our relationship. It was December 29th, 1994, and we were parked in the Chickasaw National Recreation Area Park (just talking of course). Like it was yesterday, I remember telling him I didn't think I would ever have children. His expression and response were unforgettable, and eventually led to the demise of "us." Sadly, I have seen this same look of disbelief and shock many more times since that night. But what surprised me most then, at my naïve early age, was his accusation of my selfishness. He went so far as to say that it was my God-given gift / responsibility to have children. #InsertJawDropHere

Jeremy knew I loved kids. Everyday I taught gymnastics after school and loved on those kiddos. I babysat every weekend. How could I not want to have children – he simply couldn't understand. Jeremy had never considered that a woman would make this choice, the choice to do adulting life differently. It was not natural. It was un-Godly, he told me! I am certain he didn't know the book and verse, but I have had it thrown at me repeatedly so allow me to quote it for you: "As for you, be fruitful and multiply; Populate the earth abundantly and multiply in it." Genesis 9:7 NASV. It's a commandment, right?!

Yeah, yeah, yeah, I know – go forth and multiply! Populate the earth. It's what "fulfilled and happy" women do. In another article, Pope Francis even implied that the lack of having children leads to divorce and unhappiness.[4] Maybe my desire to not have children was why my first marriage failed. #OrMaybeHeWasACheater

In July of 2015, WND ran an article titled, "Remaining Childless - Selfish or Noble." The article breaks down all the reasons women choose not to have babies, from environmental to financial reasons, and everything in between. The article ends with this:

"In the end – selfish or not – it's a personal choice for a woman whether or not to become a mother. The general hope is she doesn't achieve this status by killing any babies she 'accidentally' conceives."[5]

WOW. Selfish or not, it is a choice. I made a choice that is non-traditional. I want to empower women to make their own choice and be proud of that choice, whether it be to have 6 children and adopt another 4, or to not have children at all. If you choose to not have children – I do not condemn you. If you choose to have a child, work part-time from home, and bring the little bambino to the conferences with you – congratulations on your version of successful parenting! And if you choose to raise four children, work full-time, and volunteer as the cheerleading coach – GREAT! Do not apologize when you need to outsource house cleaning, shuttle driving, and some occasional cooking so that your weekends become about quality parenting rather than homemaking. Successful parenting may look like my friend Kelli's, Shari's, or my cousin Sarah's, and that's okay--they are all good. Today we are about redefining roles, whatever those roles might be. This freedom is empowering.

At age 40, I still have not birthed any children, and I declare it would have been very selfish of me to have had children. If I had had children that I didn't want just to fit in, then I would have been the ultimate image of selfish and self-centered. I do not apologize for choosing to be a PANK (Professional Aunt, No Kids). I do not apologize for being the best neighborhood babysitter to my friends' kids. I do not subscribe to Pope Francis's declaration that remaining childless is selfish. I strongly believe I made the right choice, and a God-directed one at that. It was my calling to consciously be a part of raising the children of my friends and relatives in the times when they need help. Today, I tell you to quit apologizing for your motherhood status, whatever it is, Mom or PANK. #PANK4life #ParentDifferently #BreakTheMold #SuccessWithoutApology

Working hard becomes a habit, a serious kind of fun. You get self-satisfaction from pushing yourself to the limit, knowing that all the effort is going to pay off.

~ Mary Lou Retton

Chapter Three
WORKING LATE

1. Do not apologize for wanting success .
2. Do not apologize for your motherhood status.

Third Commandment: Do not apologize for working late.

4. Do not apologize when you pivot.
5. Do not apologize for taking care of yourself.
6. Do not apologize for emotions (yours or others).
7. Do not apologize for friendships and loyalty.
8. Do not apologize for outsourcing.
9. Do not apologize for being the boss.
10. Do not apologize for reaping the rewards of success .

In the 1984 Olympics in Los Angeles, I discovered my first hero. When I was seven years old, I saw Mary Lou Retton compete and win a gold medal in the individual all–around competition and I was fascinated. Mary Lou Retton was the first ever American woman to win the all-around gold at the Olympics, AND the first woman to appear on a Wheaties box. Oh, how I wanted to be Mary Lou Retton. I even had my hair cut just like hers. #NotMyBestLook #ThanksGmaRow

As a young girl, Retton moved across the country in order to train for the Olympics in Houston, Texas, under Romanian coaches Béla and Márta Károlyi. Coincidentally, my mom owned a business teaching tumbling to about one hundred young boys and girls. When I was about eleven years old, and near the prime of my gymnastics career, mom took me and another aspiring gymnast to the Houston training facility to attend a gymnastics camp. We tried out to be in the next generation of super stars. After only two days of watching the girl who had been dubbed the "new Mary Lou," Kristie Phillips, I realized I was not dedicated enough for gymnastic stardom. My Olympic dreams were crushed – right then – in Houston, Texas. #InsertSadFaceHere

I didn't fear hard work. But when the girls shared their workout schedule with us, I began to comprehend the sacrifices they were making. I knew I couldn't give up my social life (and everything else) with an eye on becoming an eventual Olympic gymnast. (Oh yeah, and I was already about 6 inches too tall for an Olympic gymnast, so it was out of my hands anyway, haha.) When I look back though, I realize that as a middle school girl, I saw first-hand the dedication of young women training, sacrificing, and working hard to compete. They missed out on middle school dances, football games, cheer squads, and slumber parties; instead, they were eating, breathing, and sleeping press handstands, pivot turns, switch split leaps, and glide kips. Gymnastics wasn't the sport, the timing wasn't then, but eventually I would find the "thing" that would make the sacrifices, late nights, and social misunderstanding all totally worth it. #OlympicDreamsDieHard

As I navigated my way through high school and the first year or two of college, I sought direction; what was my goal, what would be worthy of my hard work and dedication? It wasn't until my second year of college that I at last found "it." It wasn't track and field (though I was on a track and field scholarship). It wasn't education, though I was pursuing a degree in teaching and coaching. It was this new *serious kind of fun*. I began officiating basketball games, and I loved it. Now, two decades, numerous late nights, and too-many-sacrifices-to-count later, I am committed to being the very best NCAA Division I Women's basketball referee possible. I am fully dedicated to the profession. I find great satisfaction in knowing the rules, getting the plays right, and working the game, and, come to find out, I love the late nights, the travel, and the competition.

Fifteen years into my officiating career, working a full-time job *and* in the process of buying another business, I met my second husband Jason. From our first dates, I never apologized for being gone for dinner, social events, or holidays like Thanksgiving or my birthday. I did, however, express the fact that I would not miss his special events for lack of care, but because I was a woman on a professional mission.

Traditionally a football coach, like my husband, marries a woman who is willing to center her life and career around his coaching position. Most of the older coaches, especially in pigskin country like Oklahoma and Texas, have this type of marriage. It works for them and their family. Often, their family success looks something like this: When he gets a new job, she changes jobs to follow him. When he travels for work, she finds a way to go too. When he needs clothes washed for game day, she washes and irons them. When he invites the football kids over, she cooks, cleans, serves, and loves on them like her very own kids. This is tradition, and the definition of success for so many coaching families. In their family scenario, the coach rarely, or never, apologizes for his late practices, long nights, and weekend travel. Rarely does the coach have a wife with such an independent income and schedule. Though rare, it does happen for others like it does for us, and Jason is fortunate to have had some great men who supported our non-traditional household arrangement.

In our case, I travel several nights a week. While I am gone, my husband knows where to pick up the dry cleaning, what cereal to buy, and how to clean up after himself. I do not leave lists or reminders, and I don't make it easy for him to "survive" while I am out of town. What I have learned throughout the course of our relationship and marriage is that when a woman travels, works late, and possibly earns more, the traditional roles need to be redefined. There is no "norm"—at least not a one-size-fits-all approach. So, I suggest that if you are a woman who wants to work outside the home, climb the corporate ladder, or even become an NCAA Division I basketball referee, then you need to discuss your desires and household expectations *before* marriage. You both need to understand what life looks like when a man is married to a driven, working woman. And you both need to be okay with the shared responsibilities *before* you say, "I Do." It is *THAT IMPORTANT!*

In our home the roles are shared, and WE run the household. We are responsible for the trash to be taken out, the dishes cleaned, and the lights being turned off when leaving the house. We may not be the only couple living this way, but it is still—in some places more than others--not generally the norm. If women want to be treated equally in the board room and at the office, we have to pragmatically understand how this changes our home lives too. As women, we need to rely upon partnership at home to help us succeed at work. You are not a failure if you expect your partner to buy the milk, make sure the kids brush their teeth, and place toilet paper in the powder room for company. If we expect to be equals outside the home, we must create equal partnerships inside the home. I eluded to this theme in my elevator speech, now we are digging into the details. Think about it for a moment…is your home a partnership, like a business? Like a team? If you are not married, how do you want your household to run? Do you and your significant other discuss the roles and responsibilities of the home? What are the expectations when you have children? Will one of you work less? What will happen if one of you were injured or ill? Could your partner fill in? Just take a moment and really think about your current relationship or household.

How would you categorize your home (examples of roles listed)

1. Traditional
    a. Your man is 90% responsible outside the home
    b. You are 90% responsible inside the home
    c. You handle 90% of cooking, cleaning & shopping
    d. Your man handles 75%+ of the income

2. Exhausting (Not Sustainable or Healthy)
    a. You both work outside the home
    b. You are earning near equal pay
    c. You have 90% responsibility inside the home
    d. You are primary care taker of children

3. Liberating and equal
    a. You both work outside the home
    b. Your share most duties at home
    c. You have a schedule to help each other
    d. Your partner can run the household without you if needed

Are you happy with your arrangement? Is there anything you would change?

_____
_____

How can you facilitate that change in your home?

_____
_____

Recently, a young newlywed coach asked Jason if I would speak with his new bride about being a coach's wife. He asked if I could help her understand the requirements and expectations of our role. You know—the role of the *coach's wife*. After visiting with this young couple, it was clear that when Jason brags to this young coach of my loving, wifey support, he doesn't necessarily say *how* I show my support. Consequently, when the young impressionable coach introduced his strong, independent, driven wife, I did not guide her towards a "traditional" supporting role. Instead, I shared how a liberating and equal home can support both his career and her desires of professional and independent success. I shared how Jason and I share the roles of the home and show support for one another differently than most coaching couples. With her having desires outside the home too, I encouraged them to step outside the box of traditional coach/wife roles and their engrained cultural understanding of how a 'typical' household functions. It is unclear if they will follow our advice, but I know for sure it was not the advice the young coach thought his wife was going to receive. I believe it caught him by surprise that my support didn't equate to tending solely to my husband's schedule and needs. My interest in my husband's goals and job success are equally matched by his support, sacrifices, and encouragement for my professional aspirations.

I admire the many women who have been terrific role models in terms of being the perfect "coach's wife." I expect to be a great role model too, but for a different version if you will. Because I am an example of what happens when a coach marries someone like *me* – someone who has her own agenda, her own travel schedule, and her own earnings, I can model a new look for the "supportive" wife role. I want you to know that I admire your way of supporting your partner or spouse, even if it looks traditional. You are not alone if your spousal support is different than mine. Be assured we are all just trying to figure it out – don't hate on the people who do it differently than you. Balancing the wife life and work drive, while keeping the house in order is not an easy feat. #IfItWereEasyItWouldBeAMansJob

ROLES & RESPONSIBILITIES

What does your partner/husband think of your late nights and travel? And an even deeper question: How does it impact his self esteem and identity? We are in a time in history where men are also battling with their role in the home. Women are stretching themselves thinner and thinner, doing our *please everyone* thing that we do, and men are wondering how to have purpose and fulfill the couple's partnership without being emasculated. Face it. It's true. You worry about it, and so does he. So, the question must be considered. Who is mentoring men on how to be great husbands to wives that are more driven than ever before?

Who is encouraging the men to support your late work nights by picking up the kids at daycare, preparing dinner, and cleaning up after the dog? Does your husband struggle with knowing how to support you? Does he feel appreciated by you? Does he really understand your struggle and desire to do it all, coupled with your guilt of not doing anything well enough?

> **Think about your partner's role, insecurities, strengths, and support for your success. Are you also ensuring he is receiving the support he needs to be your partner and cheerleader?**
> _____
> _____

Men and women alike have difficulty letting go of traditional, defining roles. For now, let us focus on the roles women mistakenly perpetuate, then fall short. Are you ever the mom who works the whole day, then cooks, finishes the laundry, washes the dishes, and makes a quick grocery run for the children's school supplies at the 24-hour shopping center so that no one will complain that you have to be gone the next day for a conference? You run yourself ragged because YOU feel guilty. You try to be super woman, asking for no help, saving the day at your own expense in health and sanity. I have said this before, and I will say it again: #STOPIT. That is about how bluntly my friend Stacy said it to me when she saw me waiting on my first husband hand and foot. Honestly, she probably included a few expletives in her comment, but I'll leave those to your imagination.

Stacy, my beautiful friend, is a stay-at-home mom who had once been a publishing executive. She made the choice to raise her daughters full time, rather than to work outside the home. This decision did not squelch her personal drive and competitiveness. She redirected it towards parenting and athletic competitions. Admiringly, I watched her train for and compete in triathlons, marathons, the Iron Man, and other competitions. To us outsiders, she seemed to be the perfect wife, making time to play basketball in the driveway with her girls, attend monthly dinner club, and complete training mostly while her husband was at work, all without ever complaining about being too busy or too tired.

After a few years, I finally figured out her secret—her husband! Stacy and her husband were partners. She parented while he was at work, and when she needed to train, he parented. He didn't just watch the kids, he truly *parented*: combing hair, driving the carpool to school, and maintaining discipline. If the kids needed to be fed, he did it. If they needed to be shuttled to events, appointments, or friends' houses, he did it. It was Stacy's expectation that her husband was her partner in parenting and running the household. I learned a lot from watching her. My girlfriends know Stacy did not apologize to her husband or her daughters for having her own personal desires, goals, and ambitions. If she needed to wake up at 4 am to complete a work out, she did it. If she traveled to Brazil or Atlanta or Las Vegas to compete, her husband cheered her on and encouraged her. She does "successful woman" differently, and she does so without apology. #ThanksStacy #IronManStrong

Stacy's late nights and early mornings look different from mine, but our message is the same.

- You are not a bad wife if your husband co-parents, in every sense of the word.
- You are not a bad mother if you hire a regular house cleaner.
- You are not letting your children down if you order occasional meals to your home because it makes life easier.

- If you explore your drive and ambition, your children will admire and mimic your hard work.

If you are not yet married, or haven't had children, please have these lifestyle discussions now with your significant other. Discuss your ideas about how the house should operate when you work late, or take big assignments, or want to travel a week with your girlfriends and mom. Evaluate each other's expectations in marriage. Too often, we enter marriage with an idea of what the perfect wife and mom looks like, and it doesn't match our spouse's vision.

> **What roles of the husband must change as a result of your drive and ambition? Have you two spoken about these roles?**
>
> _____
>
> _____

Or, in many cases, it is the woman who has completely unrealistic expectations for herself and her role as the perfect wife. My personal "perfect wife" used to look like some combination of Mary Ingalls (from _Little House on the Prairie_), Martha Stewart, Brooke Burke-Charvet (actor, dancer, fitness model), and Mika Brzenzinski (American television host, author, and journalist). I wanted to achieve all my goals, chase the corporate dream, make a million dollars, look hot, AND fulfill the role of the everyday homemaker by completing Pinterest projects, being a good neighbor, and having dinner on the table when he got home. I don't believe I am the only woman who had this vision of success at some point in her life. Maybe that is who you are trying to be now. Talk about unrealistic and unattainable!! As women, we can be our own worst enemy because we set unreasonable expectations for our own success. #StopIT

Don't feel like I am beating up on you; all women struggle with these unrealistic expectations. For example, the woman I mentioned above, Mika Brzezinski, is a very beautiful and intelligent journalist who co-hosts _Morning Joe,_ with Joe Scarborough, and even she admits it's a struggle. The first book she wrote, *Knowing Your Value*, had a huge impact on me after my divorce. She empowered me to aspire to and ask for equal pay. She pushed me to evaluate my worth as an employee *and* as a woman, and ask for the compensation and respect I deserved. In her book, she talks about how Morning Joe, her co-host (and now fiancé), helped her negotiate her salary. Not in a demeaning way, but in a very helpful and enlightened way; he helped her recognize the ways women tend to self-depreciate, which leads others to devalue our contributions. I was so inspired by this book I now recommend it to every woman in the workforce.

Our awareness of self-worth can be transferred to personal relationships too. As a result of Brezinski's book, I was no longer going to apologize for my successes or give others the credit for my accomplishments. If I worked all night or traveled all week to accomplish my goal, I would simply say "thank you" when complimented for a job well done. When I increased company revenue and gained expertise in new areas, I would ask for the appropriate compensation and expect to get it! In one of the last battles of my previous job, I had to fight hard for the payout for a bonus I had earned. I worked in an environment where promises were made, both verbally and in writing, that were not always expected to be upheld because of the rapid turnover of young employees. I fought for my bonus, and not surprising, the bonus for another woman in the company too. We had earned it, and I was not afraid to demand it. #KnowYourValue #AskForWhatYoureWorth

Brzezinski's first book enlightened me and changed my personal view of my life and professional worth. Her second book however proved more of a challenge for me. I have something of a love/hate relationship with this one. "Why?" Because in the second book, she implies that success at work may lead to failure at home. I guess it forced me to see that all women have periods of doubt, and sometimes very unreal expectations of ourselves and each other - even women who seem to have "made it" like Brzezinski. I thought she had figured out the perfect wife / mom / late night / early morning journalist thing, come to find out: #ShesJustLikeUs I look forward to the day that I share the stage with her at a speaking event, and I am able to tell her: you don't have to choose. Maybe this is the balance she now has with Joe. Maybe she, like me, just had to find the right partner to make it all work together for the greater good. I am confident that, Mika, you and I can each be great at work and great at home, so long as the whole family is willing to think about how the household will operate differently in this enlightened environment of equality. To Mika and each person reading this book, you are great. You are beautiful. Your children admire your hard work even in their rebellious years. If you need a little self assurance, insert your name in the following statements and say out loud _____, you are great. _____, you are beautiful. _____ your children love you and your ambition. #WomenAreCheeringForYou

A LATE NIGHT REVELATION

Have you ever had that moment when you just *knew*? You just knew something bad was about to happen, you just knew they were going to say that, or you just knew you were going to marry that guy? I had that ah-ha moment once. The moment I knew I was going to marry my husband Jason. In April 2015, I had finished five taxing and grueling months of work/life imbalance. In short, here is a brief highlight from each month.

December: Refereed out of the country for a week, and bought my first retail boutique, which required an inordinate amount of extra paperwork because the seller was not very open or cooperative.

January: I faced some tough basketball game situations which meant extra reporting and film review for the supervisors. Travel was crazy due to weather, so I also had a few long, one-way drives home in the snow (like from Fargo, North Dakota, to Oklahoma City).

February: My bosses sold the company I dearly loved, so I negotiated a six-month contract of employement with the new company (tons of uncertainty).

March: I was informed I had 30 days to relocate the new boutique due to circumstances out of my control. I was nominated to work my very first NCAA post-season tournament, which is a career dream and major goal! I began a one-year mentorship program with the George W. Bush Institute and hosted a woman from Tunisia for a week.

April: I purchased an 8,000 square foot building, a 12-person hair salon, and moved my boutique.

To say the least, I was burning the candle at both ends. I was averaging 4-5 hours of sleep, and no more than two consecutive nights were spent in the same state due to my day job and my officiating schedule. I was at an all-time high for stress, and I LOVED EVERY SINGLE MINUTE OF IT. The drive to work crazy hours is in my DNA. I knew that I was laying the groundwork, working coast to coast, for something greater, though I couldn't see the reason yet. I was taking huge leaps of faith buying the business, negotiating short term employment, etc., and I was doing it alongside Jason, whom I had been dating a few months. He was taking my calls in the middle of the night when I landed in Salt Lake City, or Sacramento, or New York City. He was picking up the mail at my house, answering group texts from my store employees, and dropping me off at the airport before sunrise. Through those 5 intense months, he was softening my hardened heart. I was falling in love with him. Yet, I wasn't ready to marry him...Until that April 17th morning!

Imagine me at my boutique desk at 5:00 am on April 17th, 2015, still working from the night before. I'd been there all night. In the last fourteen days, I had moved my boutique into my newly purchased building which was four times larger, I had worked to merge two boutique staffs, and I met all the new stylists, and my new manager. I was also proving my worth and my network to the recently installed owners of the company in NYC. On this particular morning, I had reports to email out before the 7:00 am flight, and it had taken me hours. But I was not going to miss the company-wide volunteer event in New York City. #NYCares As I peak over my desk, I see Jason asleep on the floor, waiting to take me to the airport. Yes, he had stayed all night at the store, without complaint, so he could drive me to the airport. #InsertAwwwwwsHere When I woke him, I knew. I knew HE was my life partner. Jason Melot accepted my crazy life/schedule. He wanted to do whatever it took to help me succeed. Not once since that day has he asked me for an apology for working late, working all night, or traveling to get the job done. He is proof – women can indeed have it all. #HeStillDrivesMe2TheAirport #MyBiggestFan #NotJustWhenCourtingMe

I know I am lucky. I know it is not always so simple. What are other's expectations about your time? Are you on the #SorryNotSorry treadmill with your partner, your children, or your boss? How can you reshape expectations? According to B.C. Forbes, founder of Forbes magazine, you need to *"Think not of yourself as the architect of your career, but as the sculptor. Expect to have to do a lot of hard hammering and chiseling and scraping and polishing."*

As you read my book, recognize that you are sculpting your life of success. You are doing better than you think, in part because you are facing head on this unreasonable expectation with which society has hampered you! Keep hammering and chiseling, and scraping and polishing because the next generation of women NEED you. They need your help redefining and reshaping success, even if it takes all night, or a lifetime. I am cheering for you. #SuccessWithoutApology. #LateNightsHappen

The art of life lies in a constant readjustment to our surroundings.

- Kakuzo Okakura, the Book of Tea

Chapter Four
WHEN YOU PIVOT

1. Do not apologize for wanting success .
2. Do not apologize for your motherhood status.
3. Do not apologize for working late.

Fourth Commandment: Do not apologize when you pivot.

5. Do not apologize for taking care of yourself.
6. Do not apologize for emotions (yours or others).
7. Do not apologize for friendships and loyalty.
8. Do not apologize for outsourcing.
9. Do not apologize for being the boss.
10. Do not apologize for reaping the rewards of success.

In Silicon Valley, "pivot," is arguably the most debated and overused word right now. Some naysayers think it is the new synonym for failure. In the case of my first marriage, the critics may have been right. When my Plan A thought he should sleep with other people, I was forced to take a new direction. I pivoted.

In this chapter, I will explore three reasons why women often don't pivot soon enough, and why we feel guilty when we *do* pivot, both professionally and personally.

FEAR OF CHANGE

Have you ever been to New York City's Times Square? How would you describe the scene? When you see it on television each New Year's Eve, are you amazed? I have walked through Times Square hundreds of times on the way to work. On one particular walk through Times Square though, I began to ponder my surroundings. I saw past the people and noise and noticed the massive amount of construction happening. There was scaffolding, cones, saw-horses, and caution tape everywhere. I had just walked this same street yesterday, had all these things been here then?

Who knew that Times Square needed such a massive makeover? And who knew it'd be so hard to notice the elements of this remodel during the course of the one million times I'd been there before. I had never heard anyone say, "Times Square was great, but it could use a makeover and some upgrades." Never. So why were they spending so much time and money making the GREAT square better?

Amongst the locals hustling through the crowds (whom you can always identify by their headphones and flat shoes), the tourists (identifiable by the cameras and upward staring), and the construction personnel climbing up the scaffolding, I noticed there were no signs apologizing for the inconvenience of the construction. You know, those signs you see in small business lobbies or messy airport terminals that say, "Excuse the mess while we renovate."

There were no such postings. In fact, it seems the locals expect the constant renovation, and the tourists simply look past it as though the change and progress were all part of the story told by the flashing billboards and sign tickers.

What personal lesson can we take from the constant Times Square construction and improvement? What needs renovating, upgrading, or rebuilding in your life? Often times, women, like some Silicon Valley companies, wait too late to pivot. They don't stay ahead of the need, like I saw Times Square doing that day. We don't make big changes until it becomes absolutely necessary, or we are forced. I have witnessed great women who proactively and successfully pivot in their careers. A couple famous examples: Oprah Winfrey when she left her daytime talk show to refocus on behind the camera interests, or Angelina Jolie when she left the movie business to become an international ambassador for peace. You can probably think of a few women in your own life. My mom is a great example. She owned and operated a gymnastics instruction business for 17 years, and at peak enrollment and with a state-wide reputation of excellence, she sold the business and changed careers. She knew the years ahead would not be easy. She recognized her body was not going to be as strong in the future to support and spot young athletes. She pivoted and left the hard, manual profession to focus on a career that centered more on desk work and less on muscle.

Why can't we all know when to pivot? Why can't we see the need before it is too late? I have identified four reasons--better called excuses--for why I myself don't make necessary changes in a timely manner. See if you can relate #WhyIDontPivot

1. I don't pivot because I don't notice the need.

2. I don't pivot because I fear the unknown.

3. I don't pivot because I suffer from "Others First Syndrome."

4. I don't pivot because I lack discipline.

1. #ANOTICERPROBLEM

Times Square is one of those sensory overload locations that the average person, local or tourist, can walk through and not notice any need for improvement or change. There may be light bulbs out, a sign that droops, or a better way to direct foot traffic, but the average person doesn't stop long enough to notice. Similarly, we often don't notice potential areas for improvement in our own life. We simply sail through life, eyes straight ahead, with no time for reflection. We have what I call #ANoticerProblem.

Have you ever been on a church or organizational outreach committee? When you are on such a committee, you are responsible for inviting people to the church or your organization. Some may call it an evangelism committee. Either way, when you serve on an "invite your friend" type of committee, you take ownership of first impressions. You notice the carpet stain at the front door, the hand rail in need of repair, the grumpy receptionist, or the missing letter "r" on the sign outside. Though you have entered the building in the same way for months or years without noticing these things, now they are terribly apparent! It haunts you because now you *notice*.

Changing carpet or putting back the letter "r" are easy repairs once you notice them. But what if you notice something much bigger? What if you look at your business sales and realize your favorite product on the shelf is no longer selling like it used to? What if you notice the house cleaner hasn't been changing all the sheets as scheduled? What if you notice your husband seems to be too friendly with his work associate? When will you stop long enough to notice?

I urge you to choose a regular time that allows you to stop, reflect, and really *notice* your life. Who are your friends? Who are your trusted advisors? What does the doorway to your business look like to visitors? What products do you need to stop stocking? What improvements need to be made? What can you do to be a better teacher, administrator, boss, wife, friend, or employee? What can you do to be a better *YOU?*

You cannot pivot in your personal life or your business if you don't NOTICE the need. You cannot improve your eating habits if you don't notice all the crap you put into your mouth. It's that simple. Take the time to stop and notice.

Right now: Take note of your surroundings: What could be improved to make the user, client, friend, family experience better?

_____

_____

_____

What may need change in your life – RIGHT NOW

---

2. #FEAROFUNKNOWN

Maybe you are a great noticer of things. Maybe you see the need, but fear the change. Some of my greatest regrets in my early management career came when I did not fire or release bad employees. In each case, I feared the unknown. Who would I hire to replace them? How would their friends in the company treat me if I let them go? These were the fears that ultimately delayed my decision to do the right thing for the organization and for my business. Jack Heath, author of *The Lab*, is quoted as saying, "Better the devil you know than the devil you don't." Often times, we delay change and restructuring because we do fear this devil we don't know. In fact, in almost every situation where I chose to take a new direction, the pain was less harsh than the misery of the situation before. Successful people adapt to change quickly and must not be paralyzed by their fear of the unknown.

When I noticed that my ex-husband was a cheater, I had to face my new reality. Would I stay or would I go? The unknown of single life terrified me. The devil I knew treated me well enough, earned a good living, gave me freedom, and was comfortable. The devil I didn't know has now proven to be better than I ever could have imagined. I am so thankful I didn't stay married, simply because I feared the unknown world of single life.

Franklin D. Roosevelt said in his First Inaugural Address, "The only thing we have to fear is fear itself." Are you dating a jack wagon because you fear being single? Do you fear applying for a bigger and better position because someone has said you weren't good enough? Take a moment and honestly state what you're afraid of.

What are you scared of personally?

_____

_____

What are you scared of professionally?

_____

_____

Now tell me why...

_____

_____

#WhatChangeDoYouFear

3. #OTHERSFIRSTSYNDROME

Others First Syndrome (OFS) is a made-up syndrome. I coined it because I believe it is a genuine condition. I have an employee who literally puts every single person before herself. She'll feed a stranger before she'll buy her own groceries. She'll work for free because of someone else's sad story, when she cannot pay her own bills. She has OFS in a major way. To be honest, it DRIVES ME CRAZY. I simply don't understand how she feels so obligated to help everyone else, especially, while she suffers personally.

Until, of course, I look into the mirror and realize I am doing the same thing, in my own way (I stopped long enough to notice). I help someone close a sales deal rather than work on my own deal. I help another small business do their social media instead of doing my own. I write someone else's workout plan but don't make time to work out myself. Do-gooders often are so busy doing good for everyone else they don't do good for themselves. #OthersFirstSyndrome

Mothers often hide behind the excuse of their children's needs. Remember my friend Stacy? She is the rock star mom who finds balance between training for the Iron Man and raising well-adjusted, socially active children. She does not use her children as an excuse to be out of shape. While there may be an innate desire for women to care and support others, we cannot follow it at our own expense, or this desire will lead to our demise. In what areas of your life are you making excuses because you *may* inconvenience someone else? What health regime have you not started because you are afraid it will disrupt your husband's eating habits? Are you killing yourself to serve others? If so, #STOPIT and pivot!

If you are not sure, here's an exercise for you: check your calendar for seven consecutive days. Examine every single hour. Write down whether you are working on YOUR goals, dreams, and desires, or someone else's. Be a noticer. Look, observe, and note where time is needed to advance your idea, to grow your business, or to better your marriage. I do deep studying of my time at least once a year. (John Maxwell writes great books about the value of this) When I reflect on a week and realize I spent more time, energy and brainpower on causes other than my own family income stream or personal growth, I reevaluate my commitments for the future weeks. Don't be a victim of OFS; it is a disease you can cure. #OthersFirstSyndromeCoinedFirstByMe

4. #LACKOFDISCIPLINE

We will dive deeper into this topic in future chapters, but a significant reason for not initiating change is lack of self discipline, or dare I say, laziness. If you think you have to sleep in each Saturday or Sunday, you are not disciplined enough to use that time. If you think you need to sit and watch a couple hours of television each night – your time is wasting away. If you have not exercised this week—you are lazy. It really is that simple. You are either lazy or you lack the discipline to initiate needed changes in your life. I am far from lazy, but more often than I would like to admit, I lack discipline. Each day that I chose to play Bejeweled on my phone for 30 minutes rather than editing my book was a manifestation of this lack of discipline. Each time I chose to watch Netflix on the flight rather than breakdown a game film, I was being undisciplined with my time. I loathe my lack of discipline.

When you think of the changes you need to make, ask yourself, are you disciplined enough? If you want to lose 20 pounds, are you disciplined enough to cut back on eating? If you want to have the arms of Michelle Obama, are you disciplined enough to get to the gym? If you want to write a book, will you give up other activities to commit the time to writing? Honestly, what goals in your life are out of reach because you are lazy or undisciplined? Think about your personal life and think about your business – where can you be more disciplined in order to positively impact your life?

My husband is an avid watcher of the Spike TV reality show, *Bar Rescue*. Jon Taffer, the lead in the show, is a bar consultant who goes into restaurant/bar establishments when they are losing money. He invests in renovating the space and training the bar's owners and workers. When Taffer arrives, he is asked to come help the place be profitable again. He usually renovates the look, simplifies the menu, addresses staffing concerns, and then helps reopen to the public with a new profitable model. When the show airs a few months later, the viewer gets to see the transformation and the reopening. What interests me the most though is the clip at the end of the show where they reveal how the bar is operating several months after the Taffer team leaves. Unfortunately, the bar owners often revert to their old bad habits. I don't believe the bar owners aren't smart enough, or the help not good enough. But the owners and staff are simply not disciplined enough. So in a couple of months, the bar rescue turns out to be for naught.

Are you disciplined enough to change?

Honestly answer the questions about what it takes to accomplish your goals. Then decide to be disciplined. Name one short term goal (you can measure this week or this month) that you feel you can accomplish by simply being disciplined in a good habit.

Goal: _____

_____

Discipline Required to Accomplish Goal: _____

_____

Now tell me, can you pivot from your wasteful activities? Can you make more permanent changes necessary for accomplishing your larger long-term goals? Do you need some positive affirmations? I have listed four affirmations for you here.

1. I <u>notice</u> the need for change. The change I can make today is ___

_____

2. I do not fear the unknown.

3. I will not neglect myself for the sake of placing others first.

4. I am disciplined enough to _____

_____

You can also download more affirmations from my website www.successwithoutapology.com.

I love watching people improve their life. I mean I love, love, love watching people achieve their version of success. From Jessie in NYC, who is trying to chase her dream of being a fashion marketer, to Madi in Oklahoma, who is developing her photography business, to Missy in Missouri, who is flipping homes and finding love again...I love when people call to tell me about their success. That is why this book means so much to me. I believe in you. I believe in your ability to accomplish your goals. I am cheering for your success, and I don't want you to look back or apologize when you attain it. #SuccessWithoutApology

I try to love people right where they are, which is a skill I observed in my father. But I also love people who show me where they want to be, who they want to be, and what they want to do. When a woman tells me of her plan for improvement, then shares with me the small achievements, I am happy to my core! Do you have people in your life with whom you share your successes and accomplishments? Sometimes that one person may be your mentor or best friend or husband. This person is your cheerleader, your "atta-girl" friend. I have a couple of these people in my life. In my basketball world, Bob has been my cheerleader for almost a decade, and now my husband is a great supporter and cheerleader too. In my new public speaker and authorship role, I have Shirin and Sandy. They are the two I pick up the phone and share my baby accomplishments with, and they clap and cheer and then ask what goal is next. I love my cheerleaders!! Because let's be real folks, change takes time, and sometimes we get impatient. Our encouragers often keep us motivated, positively inspired, and on track.

Do you remember the 1980's game, the Rubik's Cube? It frustrated many a Gen-Xer back in the day. We were unable to get all the same colored cubes on the same side (unless, of course, we took the stickers off and replaced them). After completing a side or even two to be a solid color, the final sides could not be completed without undoing some of the completed two sides. This process is true of any major pivot. The perfectly fine, comfortable and easy, has to be disrupted. When you notice the need to pivot, people will be uncomfortable. When you stop drinking for greater health, some people will not understand. When you stop going out for lunch because you are budgeting, people may ridicule you. When you renovate the office, people will complain. Great change requires self-discipline and the confidence to know that some discomfort will be required.

As I write this book, I am mid-pivot with my hair salon. When I purchased the salon, it had twelve booth-paying professionals. There were 11 stylists and one nail technician. Most of the stylists had been at this location together for about a decade, after staging a mass exodus from another salon. Unfortunately, this group had a major fear of the unknown. As soon as I purchased the salon, the ring-leader of the group began fueling their fears with unsubstantiated rumors and claims. For too long I tried to ignore, downplay, or deny the poison of negativity in the group. #TheDevilIKnew

For almost a year, the group leader led an underground negativity campaign, fostering distrust and anxiety. Though complimentary of my operation, hard work and attentiveness, behind my back, they wanted me to fail. Even the manager *on my payroll*, began to believe their rumors and lies. She began doubting the salon's future and informed me the ring-leader was planning another mass exodus at an undisclosed date. #JustWhatIneededNOT So, I had a massive decision to make. Should they stay or should they go? I thought back to all my previous leadership roles. #TheDevilIDidntKnow

I reflected on the advice of a consultant who once counseled our church when it was in the midst of some unrest. The consultant explained it is Five times harder to make an unhappy church member happy than it is to recruit a new member. Let me say this again, while you think about your employees, your business, or your membership through this lens: **"It is Five times harder to make an unhappy member happy, than it is to recruit a new member."** Restructuring was inevitable for my salon, but I had to decide if I wanted to try and win over those consumed by negativity, or simply cut my ties and face the unknown.

As scary as it was both for my finances and my reputation, I believed my salon business would be healthier if I chose to release the toxic, unhappy people. After counsel from others and a lot of prayer, I notified everyone who wanted to leave they could go. Anyone who chose to stay would be a part of a new environment and the boss-bashing would come to an immediate end.

As suspected, 7 great stylists walked out the door, most of them mad as hell, and a couple of them scared about their future. Each woman who left was great at her craft, and most were also great people. Unfortunately, the leadership of one naysayer, and their collective fear of the unknown, prevented them from being happy with the change in salon ownership. #NoWinSolution

My pocket book, and my reputation as a salon owner were going to take a hit when they left, but to complete this Rubik's Cube I was going to have to shake up the one seemingly perfect side to solve the complete puzzle. I do not minimize the difficulty of this emotional and tough decision, but it was time for the salon to pivot. In this scenario, I noticed the problem, recognized the need for change, and had to make drastic decisions, as scary as they might have been. As I mentioned, now I am mid-pivot, recruiting more stylists and cultivating a new teamwork environment with my current staff. Though slow and somewhat painful, it truly is 5x easier to recruit new stylists than it would have been to make those who didn't want to be there happy. #ByeFelicia #ChangeIsGood

Now that I am filling my salon with stylists full of joy, energy, and excitement, I hope you gain confidence from this chapter. I had to pivot, and do so hard and fast, but it has worked to my advantage. Have the confidence in yourself to do what you know to be right, and do it without apology! I know these decisions are never easy. So be sure to prepare.

Take the time to reflect.

Pray about it.

Seek council.

Then pivot if necessary.

Physical fitness is not only one of the most important keys to a healthy body, it is the basis of dynamic and creative intellectual activity.

-John F. Kennedy

Chapter Five
TAKING CARE OF YOURSELF

1. Do not apologize for wanting success (being focused and driven).
2. Do not apologize for your motherhood status.
3. Do not apologize for working late.
4. Do not apologize when you pivot.

Fifth Commandment: Do not apologize for taking care of yourself.

6. Do not apologize for emotions (yours or others).
7. Do not apologize for friendships and loyalty.
8. Do not apologize for supporting other women.
9. Do not apologize for being the boss.
10. Do not apologize for reaping the rewards of success.

Successful people value themselves highly, and they want to be present. They invest in their well-being. If you want to be amongst the most successful people, then healthy choices are not optional. This is a chapter about more than a low number on the scale, but it's worth noting that according to the Center for Disease Control (CDC), employees who are overweight take more sick days than their healthier weight colleagues.[6] On average, overweight and obese employees miss anywhere from an additional two days to a full WEEK of work compared to employees at a healthy weight. When was the last time you took a sick day from work? How many sick days do you take each year? When was the last time your boss took a sick day? You can make all the excuses you want for being regularly sick, but have you looked at your personal weight as one of the reasons?

To be sick and miss out on something just kills me. If I am at home sick, I know I am not getting ahead in life. Knowing that peak performance requires health, we have to be committed to a healthy weight, without apology. It is paramount to our success to be disciplined in the care of our bodies. Have you ever noticed that the most successful people seem to be nearly invincible against tiredness, sickness, or unhappiness? They always appear to have it together. Because, like Mr. Kennedy, uber successful people feel that physical, mental and emotional health is largely within our control. Whatever time, money, or effort it takes to maintain your health is justified. When you look at your day, do you schedule exercise? Do you set aside time for mental or physical health? Are you at a healthy weight? If not, why not? What excuses are you making for your unhealthy lifestyle?

Without a doubt, I am guilty! I make excuses such as:

- I am only in NYC occasionally, so I have to go eat the best food.
- I only see her occasionally, so I have to go meet her for drinks.
- I am too tired.
- I worked late.
- My feet hurt, or my knees ache.

I know I cannot and will not work out if I wait until after work. So early mornings are my "healthy" time. This is when I plan my meals, read my devotion, and exercise. Resisting the urge to jump on my phone first thing in the morning, I try to stop long enough to sneak away for 45 minutes to work out and eat breakfast. To maintain focus throughout the day and to stay balanced, I begin my day with scheduled, intentional personal health time, even if it means getting up super early.

Successful women enjoy all that life entails (work and play), and they simply can't afford to have excessive illness or injury to disrupt this trajectory. But maybe you are not convinced that "being successful" is reason enough to have a healthy body. Try any one of these reasons: swimsuit season, class reunion, new job, interview, wedding, family pictures, your children, holiday party, the list goes on. Ultimately, I want to encourage you to be healthy for the most important reason of all: YOU. There is no better person or reason to be healthy than you, your goals, your life. Right now I want you to decide to be the healthiest version of yourself. Start today. Make a vow to be healthier today than you were yesterday.

If you don't know where to begin, or you simply want some encouragement, I will share SIX SIMPLE AND LIFE-CHANGING HABITS I implement in my life. I believe they are basics to becoming a thriving, successful woman. Personalize these habits and adapt them to your life to ensure your mind, body and soul are healthy enough for success. #CantGetAheadIfYouAreHomeSick

#1 SIMPLE AND LIFE-CHANGING HABIT: GET UP!

When the alarm goes off and the voice of the devil tells you that five more minutes won't hurt, DON'T LISTEN! That is the voice of the average; the voice of the unmotivated; the voice of those whom you leave behind. You must put mind over mattress. #MindOverMattress

Did you know that if you get up one hour earlier each morning you gain 15 more days per year? That's right. Ask me how I get so much accomplished. I'll answer, "because my year has 380 days and yours only has 365." #EarlyBirdGetsTheWorm #15MoreDays

Successful people do not sleep until 2 pm on Saturday, or even 11 am; they get up. Many keep the same schedule on the weekend that they have during the week. Just think about it, if you are awake at 7 am on Saturday, you may have a head start on everyone else for the weekend fun, the family time, or the feast cooking! This has become habit for my husband and me. We do not linger in bed, even on our day off. We get up and get going.

#2 SIMPLE AND LIFE-CHANGING HABIT: DRINK WATER!

Everyone needs to drink more water. It's a given. Not soda. Not iced tea. Just plain, ole water. I don't need to give you all of the scientific data here because I'm sure you have heard it all before. But how about the fact that if you lose even 1.5% of your body's H2O, you are at the tipping point of mild dehydration, thereby causing your mood, energy levels, and cognitive function all to drop. Think about it like this, less water = less energy; less water = less brain power; less water = worse mood.

Many women are susceptible to dehydration without knowing it. For example, an article in Health mentions these risk factors for dehydration:

- Diabetic
- On your period
- Taking prescription medications (like blood pressure medication)
- On a low carb diet
- Are pregnant
- Fly often
- Taking vitamin supplements
- Live /work in high altitude
- Drink alcohol

When your body needs water – your brain needs help. So drink up. #DrinkWater #StopPop

#3 SIMPLE AND LIFE-CHANGING HABIT: EXERCISE YOUR BODY!

Yes, I said it, you gotta exercise. And if you don't believe me, look at the exercise habits of any of these very successful people. If you do not have a job that allows you to move naturally as you work, then you have to intentionally find time to work out or go to the gym. I cite Andrew Merle's blog post on the exercise habits of uber-successful people.

- Barack Obama, former President of the United States: Exercises for 45 minutes a day, six days per week. He exercises first thing in the morning, alternating between lifting weights one day and doing cardio the next.

- Anna Wintour, Vogue editor-in-chief: Wakes up at 5:45 a.m. so she can play an hour of tennis every morning.

- Condoleeza Rice, former U.S. Secretary of State: Gets up at 4:30 a.m. to get in 40 minutes of cardio, usually on a treadmill or elliptical machine.

- Mark Cuban, owner of the NBA's Dallas Mavericks: Does an hour of cardio per day, 6-7 days a week. He does the elliptical and stair gauntlet, plays basketball, and takes kickboxing and other aerobic classes at the gym.

- Tim Cook, CEO of Apple: Wakes at 4:30 a.m. and hits the gym several times per week. He also enjoys cycling and rock climbing.

- Richard Branson, founder of Virgin Group: Wakes as early as 5 a.m. to kite surf, swim, or play tennis in the morning. He claims he gets four hours of additional productivity every day by keeping up with his consistent exercise schedule.

Everyone's doing it. #PeerPressureStrikesAgain You don't have to do your workout in the morning, but you have to work out regularly. Although you may have noticed most of the people mentioned above choose to exercise in the morning. Which points me back to daily habit number one – GET UP! Get up, drink water, and exercise. #SimpleHabits

#4 SIMPLE AND LIFE-CHANGING HABIT: READ!

Successful people read. In an opinion piece by Andrew Merle in the *Observer*, he mentions Bill Gates, Mark Cuban, Elon Musk and Oprah Winfrey and their reading habits. Merle says it matters not only that you read, but what you read. See this excerpt from his article:

"In fact, there is a notable difference between the reading habits of the wealthy and the not-so-wealthy. According to Tom Corley, author of *Rich Habits: The Daily Success Habits of Wealthy Individuals*, rich people (annual income of $160,000 or more and a liquid net worth of $3.2 million-plus) read for self-improvement, education, and success. Whereas poor people (annual income of $35,000 or less and a liquid net worth of $5,000 or less) read primarily to be entertained."

Do you read to learn or read to be entertained? Let's do a little quiz:

1. What was the last book you read for learning?
2. What was the last piece you read for entertainment?
3. How often do you read for learning? (like now)
4. How often do you read for entertainment?
5. How much time did you spend reading for improvement and success this month?

I confess. I do not have $3.2 million+ in liquid net worth (yet). But because I want to, I get up, I drink water, I exercise, and I read. There is always a self-improvement book in my bag, purse or backpack. If you would like a few reading suggestions, try these.

- *The 7 Habits of Highly Effective People* by Stephen Covey
- *Know Your Value* by Mika Brzezinski
- *Who Moved My Cheese* by Dr. Spencer Johnson
- *The Purpose Driven Life* by Rick Warren
- *Lean In* by Sheryl Sandberg
- *Outliers* by Malcom Gladwell
- *Conscious Business: How to Build Value Through Your Values* by Fred Kofman

#5 SIMPLE AND LIFE-CHANGING HABIT: GIVE!

Everyday people who give, become successful people who give. Tom Corley, author of *Wealthy Habits: The Daily Success Habits of Wealthy Individuals*, states that 73% fo the 233 wealthy people he studied for five years, volunteer 5+ hours a month. Bill Gates, Marie Forleo, Oprah Winfrey, and Mark Zuckerberg all donate to multiple causes.

Andrew Carnegie was once quoted as saying, "No man can become rich without himself enriching others." Ted Turner, former CEO of Turner Broadcasting System (TBS) and vice chairman and director of AOL Time Warner, has a net worth estimated to be $2.1 billion. His lifetime donations are considered to be more than half of that, at $1.2 billion. #HolyGenerousGiving

Wealth-X, a firm that does research and valuations on ultra-high net worth individuals, gives Turner a Generosity Index of 57%, which is super high. Whatever your worth, have you ever been in a position to charitably GIVE AWAY 57% of it?

If you want my current reading list, which includes both fiction and non-fiction - you can email me anytime or follow me on Goodreads. @RachaelMelot

The habit of giving is innate to some children, but for many of us it is a learned behavior. My grandfather was a giver; all 95 years of his life he gave unto others abundantly. My mother is now a giver, just like her father. And I hope to be remembered as a giver. As a result of witnessing my mom give to those less fortunate, or those who were hurting, I learned invaluable giving habits. We must teach our children to give with an open and loving heart. A giving heart is a prosperous one!

#6 SIMPLE AND LIFE-CHANGING HABIT: BE PRESENT!

Multi-tasking is so 2012! It is time to stop carrying two phones, answering work emails while at your child's piano recital, and texting responses back to your mom while driving and eating lunch. When interviewed by a local paper for a feature article, headlined the "ultimate multi-tasker," I responded to the question of "How do you accomplish so much in such a variety of fields?" And my answer then was the same as it is now: I work hard to be present. I believe you can accomplish more if you give the task at hand your full attention. So be present.

When I am with my girlfriends, enjoying our monthly dinner out, I put my phone away and talk to them. I laugh at their jokes and cry for their sadness. I hug them and love them and spend face-to-face, eye-to-eye time talking. I am present.

The greatest gift you can give your friends, your family, or your business is your genuine presence. When I am officiating a basketball game, I cannot be thinking about the store's profit & loss statement—I must be laser focused. When I am working on a marketing campaign for the launch of a new product, I must give my creative staff my full, undivided attention so that I can efficiently evaluate ideas and delegate tasks. This is the hardest of all the habits, but it can have a substantial impact on your productivity and personal relationships. #BePresent2BeGreat

I am not your trainer, your psychologist, or your therapist, but I know these six easy habits will change your life for the better.

GET UP!

DRINK WATER!

EXERCISE YOUR BODY!

READ!

GIVE!

BE PRESENT!

Reflecting on this chapter, truly ask yourself: when was the last time you read a book or exercised just for you? When did you turn off your cell phone to simply sit and listen to your children talk about their day? Did you apologize for taking "me" time?

Today, take some time to read before you go to bed. Spend an extra 15 minutes just hanging out with your husband after dinner. Be present. If you are not already in the habit of doing these six healthy ways of life, claim them now as your new habits. Vow to make this year better. Then pay it forward by encouraging all of your employees and peers to make healthy lifestyle choices. And do not apologize for taking care of yourself. I repeat. Do not apologize for taking care of yourself.

I learned long ago, never to wrestle with a pig.
You get dirty, and besides, the pig likes it.

George Bernard Shaw

Chapter Six
EMOTIONS

1. Do not apologize for wanting success (being focused and driven).
2. Do not apologize for your motherhood status.
3. Do not apologize for working late.
4. Do not apologize when you pivot.
5. Do not apologize for taking care of yourself.

Sixth Commandment: Do not apologize for emotions (yours or others).

7. Do not apologize for friendships and loyalty.
8. Do not apologize for supporting other women.
9. Do not apologize for being the boss.
10. Do not apologize for reaping the rewards of success.

I may be a farmer's daughter, but I didn't understand this quote until I got in the mud with a real-life pig of a man. Take a lesson from my life and stay far, far away from the cute, little piggy. While this is not a chapter on marriage, my past experience will set the stage for how I became unapologetic for my emotions. Be prepared…this gets a bit personal.

A typical Monday morning routine for me in 2012:

3 a.m. Alarm

4 a.m. Leave house

5 a.m. Arrive at airport

6 a.m. American Airlines flight departs OKC airport (with me asleep in a window seat).

After a brief plane change in Dallas, I land in New York City for a week of hustle. On this particular Monday morning, I missed my flight. It's okay; I missed it on purpose. My husband was unusually attentive and talkative for 3 a.m.—therefore, New York City could wait. I sat on the edge of the bed an extra 45 minutes to soak in the much-needed attention from him. You see he was not an affectionate man. He grew up without a lot of affection in his family, and he didn't give it freely, even to me.

Looking back, I felt anxiety about leaving this particular morning. I mean, I had been making this trip every other week for about two years, but this time seemed different. On the drive to the airport, I attributed my anxiety to my own insecurity. I was feeling unattractive and a bit blue since returning from our very unaffectionate, ten-year anniversary trip to San Francisco the prior week. I craved more. I desperately desired my husband's touch. So, on this one early morning, when he paid attention to me – my world paused long enough to relish the feeling (and miss the flight). #715flightwillworktoday

Landing in New York City about 1:00 p.m., my first inbound phone call came while I was still seated on the plane. I'll never forget leaning forward, resting my elbows on my knees while listening to my friend. She said my husband, whom I was still thinking about, was caught texting another woman, and worse, professing his love to her. My ex was having ANOTHER affair. I hung up the phone, walked off the plane and just leaned against the hard, cold LaGuardia airport wall. I was in shock. This morning, what was that? Did I imagine his adoration? How long had he been cheating on me *this time*? Was I so unlovable? Those questions rattled my mind and nothing but self-doubt surfaced. A mere 14 days after our anniversary, my heart was crushed. This was not his first affair, but this would be his last. I will never forget that moment when I said, *no more*. This is over; as Carrie Underwood so defiantly crooned, "Next time it won't be on me." He had cheated on me before, and I had chosen to stay married. That was on me. I am sure there were several reasons, my traditional upbringing, my emotions of fear, my desire to make him happy, but whatever all those reasons were before, they no longer mattered. This time it most definitely would not be on me. I was done. It was time I stopped wrestling with a pig.

WHAT NOW?

All I could think was, *what now?* Where did I go wrong? Why couldn't I make him happy? I worked hard. I loved sex (though he often told me no). I paid the bills. I supported his golf hobby. I kept the house clean. What else could I do to make this man, or any man, happy? What was I doing wrong? #HowDidIFail

In my mid-thirties, married, working a great job, officiating college basketball and then... this "trigger" moment happened – I would be divorced and alone. In a matter of moments, my self-image became that of a desperate singles ad, reading something like this:

Not the prettiest, divorced, middle-aged workaholic female executive (probably a bitch). Not that skinny, but works out. No children – probably something wrong. Drinks a little. Travels too much. Really religious, and cusses like a sailor. #GoodLuckFindingAMate

Yes, that is exactly what I thought of myself, and subsequently, I feared people's perceptions. The loss of my security blanket, a.k.a. marriage, rocked my world. I was a divorcee. How the hell did this happen? Would I be forever labeled as the woman who chose her career over family? Would I ever recover financially or emotionally from this? Who am I now? What am I supposed to do? Where am I supposed to live? How come I couldn't make him happy? #IWasLost

HIS EMOTIONS

After I filed for divorce, my husband and I had a couple of heart-to-heart conversations along the lines of *how did we get here?* What I learned is that my husband chose to keep his emotions to himself. He chose to hide his insecurities and his depression. He never gave me that desperately needed insight into his psyche; therefore, I was blind to his emotional needs. I told him, and am sharing with you, that he chose to solve his emotional problems with his penis rather than with his wife. That was HIS choice. He felt sad, so he cheated. He felt lonely, so he cheated. He felt inferior, so he cheated. #HisCheatingIsNotMyFault

Let me tell you, if you are a woman with a cheating husband, IT IS NOT YOUR FAULT. Your success is not the reason for his insecurity or unhappiness. It took a great deal of counseling (some professional) and soul searching to accept the fact that I was not responsible for his emotions. My husband's affairs were not my fault. I do not apologize for his cheating. I do not apologize for his emotional instability. While I could have sympathized with his emotions, I could not change them. They were his feelings. Unfortunately, rather than solving his emotional needs with me, he did it, secretly, outside of our relationship. When he sabotaged our marriage by seeking solace outside our marriage, he knew he was wrong. When discussing divorce, he told me I did not do anything wrong, nor did he expect me to apologize for my drive and ambition. So when society, friends, and acquaintances said he cheated because I am an ambitious and busy woman, I called BS. I refuse to accept that accusation. I was broken, insecure, hurt, and betrayed, but I was not going to apologize for my professional success, nor was I going to allow people to convince me it was my fault. #HisCheatingIsNotMyFault

MY EMOTIONS

In business, women are sometimes stereotyped as emotional or dramatic, and because of that, they often try to stifle their personal feelings in the workplace. In the past, I rarely showed my raw emotions at work, but that is because my opinion on women's emotions has changed in recent years. I believe women are tough and resilient and can actually use their emotions to drive success. Now I believe women can use their feelings, fears, and ambitions to spur professional focus and success. The year following my divorce, I worked further in post-season basketball than ever before; made more money than ever before, and I bought my first corporation. I was on a mission to fill the void and used my emotions to my advantage. I shared my struggles with a few people, and now I understand that my emotions were my strength. They were not my weakness. I no longer apologize for making decisions based, partially, on my emotional needs.

In a few short years after my divorce, I redefined my image. I show my emotions more freely, with both my peers and my employees. I believe the openness and vulnerability comes with confidence, and some life experience. I am no longer the desperate, scared, divorced woman whose husband left her. I am a successful, faith and joy-filled woman who scrapped her way back to happiness. I daily work on my legacy, and who I am today is who I wish I would have become sooner. Who I will be tomorrow, I hope continues to be better than who I was today. Part of my journey is to increase my emotional intelligence (EI), for myself and for others. Are you using your emotions to grow your success and your legacy or are you using your emotions, or the emotions of others to cripple your progress? Our emotions are powerful tools if you can figure out how to use them. Research EI to further hone this skill.

If you work on your emotional intelligence, as I did, you begin to:

- recognize and label your own emotions
- recognize and label other's emotions
- use emotions to guide behavior
- adjust emotions and adapt to environments to achieve personal goals

Emotional intelligence (EI) is the capability of individuals to recognize their own, and other people's emotions, to discriminate between different feelings and label them appropriately, to use emotional information to guide thinking and behavior, and to manage and/or adjust emotions to adapt environments or achieve one's goal(s).

Emotional intelligence is very much a type of "smarts" that we can continue to learn, and, in the process, show signs of maturity. When you are able to identify and label your emotions, you are able to control them and use them more wisely for personal and professional success. Referees, like myself, work on this every game, in every situation. We must be able to recognize the emotions of players, coaches, and our partners by the simplest of verbal and non-verbal cues. For example, a referee may recognize that the point guard is feeling frustrated by the full court pressure of the other team. If this point guard isn't handling the pressure very well, she may make a bad pass or not properly set up the offense, which in turn causes the coach to react. It is our job as referees, to recognize the cause and effect of this defensive pressure on the point guard. We need to be in great position to see any illegal contact between the point guard and the defender, as well as be aware the coach may request a time out to regroup or restructure the offense. We must "feel" the emotions change on the court and put ourselves in the best possible position to make good decisions for the game, the player, and the coach.

When we are able to communicate effectively in response to multiple types of emotions, we are more successful. This has become a great life skill for me. As others become more irrational and allow their own emotions to overcome their logic, I generally become calmer. I attribute this skill to my 20+ years of officiating and calmly dealing with emotional coaches and players. #Key2Success

If you become your best self because of your worst experience, or rawest emotions, I applaud you; you will have a story to share. And as I introduced this chapter as not-a-marriage-chapter but one on self-awareness and emotional empowerment, I want to bring you full circle to the point of #SuccessWithoutApology and emotions.

Remember two thoughts:

1. IQ may get you hired, but EI will get you promoted.
2. You don't need to apologize for your emotions, or anyone else's, but you do need to understand them, regulate them, and sometimes use them for motivation.

Who are you allowing to affect your emotions negatively?

_____

_____

Who are you allowing to affect your emotions positively?

_____

_____

How can you increase your emotional intelligence? How can more emotional intelligence help you attain your personal goals?

_____

_____

Some women pray for their daughters to marry good husbands. I pray that my girls will find girlfriends half as loyal and true as the Ya-Yas.

— Rebecca Wells, *Divine Secrets of the Ya-Ya Sisterhood*

Chapter Seven
FRIENDSHIPS AND LOYALTIES

1. Do not apologize for wanting success (being focused and driven).
2. Do not apologize for your motherhood status.
3. Do not apologize for working late.
4. Do not apologize when you pivot.
5. Do not apologize for taking care of yourself.
6. Do not apologize for emotions (yours or others).

Seventh Commandment: Do not apologize for friendships and loyalty.

8. Do not apologize for supporting other women.
9. Do not apologize for being the boss.
10. Do not apologize for reaping the rewards of success.

Being privy to the laughter between two of the most opposite women you can imagine was what I loved about hanging with mom and her best friend Kathy. Though mom had several good friends, Kathy remained my favorite through my teenage years. She was mom's crazy friend, the liberal transplant from California. Kathy taught ballet, tap dance and jazz in our little town, and when she first started the business, she partnered with my Mom who ran the tumbling, gymnastics, and ribbon classes for her. They were the best of friends, using each other's experiences to start their own small business, a business that shaped the lives of thousands of young girls and boys.

When I say they were opposites, I mean in almost every conceivable way. Kathy is about 5'2", mom is closer to 5'9". Kathy was married to a biker-type guy, had wild curly hair, one son, and couldn't care less about what others thought of her. My mom was married to a cowboy, had super straight short hair, and was raising 4 young children. I remember fun "Aunt" Kathy as being creative, artistic, stylish, aloof and loyal. She showed me how to find costumes and outfits at thrift stores, and she had the biggest closet I had ever seen! Her views were considered liberal and sometimes more risqué than our little Oklahoma town was ready to embrace, but Kathy never apologized or complained about being different. She just owned it - as opposed to my mom who never wanted to be an outsider. She jumped into every Bible Study group, church luncheon, and civic organization in her efforts to assimilate as a local. The differences between mom and Kathy taught me a key friendship lesson: best friends can pursue success and happiness differently.

In this chapter, I will celebrate friendships and loyalty, admit my challenges of finding and maintaining girlfriends, and celebrate the health benefits of friendship. Successful women need not apologize for friendship time. If you don't recall the last time you spent a couple hours just hanging with the girls, schedule some time right now. #RightNow

Socializing with friends is proven to be an important component of a healthy, long life. Okinawans, for example, have Moais, or social support groups, formed to provide varying life support. Moai means "meeting for a common purpose" in Japanese. Research suggests Moais contribute to longevity in the Okinawan people. Similiar to their Moais, I have my local dinner club of support, and a great referee friendship circle. Do you have a group of friends who frequently meets for the common purpose of socializing? Who are your three best friends? When are you scheduled to meet with them next? #RightNow

Socializing has a measurable result on health. Brigham Young University researchers claim people with stronger social relationships have a 50 percent greater chance of survival than those who don't possess these types of connections. During times of high stress, unfortunately our friendships can fade into the background, if not consciously maintained. Letting friendships fall to the wayside is a mistake and in fact, counterproductive to maintaining your physical, mental and emotional well-being! Stop apologizing for your girl's night out and your regularly scheduled happy hour. Celebrate the fact that friendships are great for your health. #IWillToast2That #FriendsMatter

Despite popular opinion, girls can do more than just gab and drink wine. Kathy and my mom were also my first female entrepreneurial heroes. In the early 1980's, when women were not running as many businesses, both Mom and Kathy built up small ventures that eventually supported them and their family. My mom and Kathy initially taught their classes in an old armory building, only a block from my elementary school. Mom's office was the equipment closet, in a dated structure with no air conditioning or heat, just concrete floors and a few garage doors to circulate air. The armory building was actively operated and used, so when the army carried out their drills one weekend each month, all the dance bars and gymnastics mats, beams, and equipment had to be taken up, stored for the weekend, and then brought back out after military drill weekend ended. My mom, with the assistance of four very helpful children, broke down and stowed away the equipment every few weeks. I learned how to work for what I wanted, without complaining about the details.

As their friendship blossomed, so did their businesses. So much so, they eventually split their companies and each bought their own facility. I find it so amazing now, how they could have been business partners, disagree about their futures, and still remain friends. Mom and Kathy demonstrated true friendship.

Throughout the duration of their business partnership, I did not witness my mom and Kathy actually argue, though they disagreed (and sometimes very strongly I later found out). As friends, I saw them laugh so hard they'd cry, hug when they had no words, and hold each other up when the other was hurting. I liken them to the quote from Shannon A. Thompson, in *Death Before Daylight*. "Watching them was like watching the sunset and the sunrise, equally beautiful in different ways."

When interviewing Mom for details for this chapter, I learned there was more to the story when they split their businesses – and some disagreements that were tough for them. It wasn't just growth, as I had thought as a child. It was a difference of opinion as to where to move the businesses as they grew. In fact, the growth and business separation was very tough for a few months. Mom says she's so thankful they didn't have social media then because in today's digital age, their personal friendship and business may have become other people's business. In the pre-Facebook era, they were able to work it out together and remain friends. They handled their matters intimately by getting mad, then apologizing and forgiving. They went back to being best friends, who did business separately. To this day, Mom and Kathy have endured all of life's highs and lows with an unconditional love. That is the friendship every successful woman should work to have.

FINDING FRIENDS: CHILDHOOD

In the first grade, our parents carpooled us to school; she was such a fun friend. As soon as we arrived on the playground though, she became the bully and I her victim. Her bullying continued off and on until I was in high school and it really affected my entire friendship circle. You see we grew up in a small town, so when she ridiculed me in elementary school, threatened to kill me in middle school, and pursued (and kissed) my boyfriend in high school, everyone knew. I was a star athlete, excelled in the classroom, knew and hung out with everyone, but couldn't really figure out how to make close friends.

For any young woman who knows the feeling and hasn't found great girlfriends yet, don't be discouraged. My sophomore year in high school is when I made my first lifelong, dear friend. Our friendship, sadly, developed because we each experienced the tragic loss of a sibling while in high school. Her sister died in a car accident and almost one year later, my little brother took his own life. #TragedyInaSmallTown #RIPElainaAndJohnJacob

Mourning the loss of a sibling together built an unbreakable friendship foundation. Rather than being needy teenagers, we had grieving parents who needed us to be strong. Our evaluation of what was important in life changed, our relationship with our parents was strained, and our connection became one of the first true, unconditional friendships in my life. Now, though still bullied, I didn't care. I had a new perspective on life, and I began to trust Erin and a few other girls with all of my emotions. I learned through this tragedy to be vulnerable and to allow girls, especially Erin, to become true friends. To this day, 20+ years later, she and I can lounge around and laugh, cry, grieve, and reminisce like no time has passed. I treasure her friendship and our history. If I lived any closer to her today, I promise I would be in her Bunko group and she would be a member of our dinner club! #FriendsForever #GodsPlan

FINDING FRIENDS: COLLEGE

Huddling on the stairwell taking our group kinesiology test, downing vodka shots on each base of the diamond, attending chapel each Wednesday, and eating convenience store burritos and corn dogs on her father's gas card, is how I bonded with my next lifelong friend. Charla and I can still laugh for two days straight recalling our college memories, some of which we may deny to our parents, ha! To this day, Charla is one of my first calls when I need prayer, when I hear certain songs from the 90's, and when I want to talk about someone from our college days. Through intentional long distance communication, we continue to grow closer. We have shared many adulthood pains, sorrows, and joys. In college, I found my second life-long friend. #UntoldStoriesAtCollege

FINDING FRIENDS: ADULTHOOD

After college graduation, I was a working girl in desperate need of a local girlfriend. Erin was in California (high school friend), Charla was in Missouri (college friend), and Meredith had moved an hour away (first job friend). I was in a lonely marriage and desperately desired the kind of girl friendship my mom had with Kathy. I needed my Moai, my daily support group of girlfriends. When I learned of another woman's dinner club, I decided I wanted one of those. So, as any good entrepreneur would do, I researched dinner clubs and determined I could establish my own. #Entrepreneurship #IfYouWantItBuildIt

My dinner club goal: draw up a dinner club format that fostered girls-only loyalty, openness, fun and privacy for busy, motivated and driven women in need of friendship as much as me.

Six women accepted my invitation to join the dinner club – though they all told me later they were very skeptical! Similar to the feeling of releasing this book to the public, I had to let go of my inhibitions and insecurities and simply go for it. In 2006, we met for the first time and have met almost every single month for the last eleven years. Now, I have my personal Ya-Ya Sisterhood, and these women are my strength, my encouragement, and my Moai. I am so thankful for Angie, Audrey, Danielle, Erika, Kelli, Leigh-Anne, Melissa, Misty, Shari and Stacy. We have a unique friendship and firm commitment to attending our girl time! If you want to create a dinner club you can use some of our rules listed on my website rachaelmelot.com. #BecauseOfCourseIhaveRules #DinnerClub4Life #OurYaYaSisterhood

The last decade, we have supported each other through marriages, anniversaries, divorces, deaths, surprises, business ventures, births, new jobs, lawsuits, lay-offs, moves and so much more. We have loved, laughed and cried, taken road trips, rented limos, floated rivers, attended concerts, and baby-sat for one another. We are the Ya-Ya Sisterhood I dreamed of, the Moai proven to extend life and health. I honestly don't believe I would have such a successful life without them. #SuccesfulWomenNeedGirlfriends

As women take on more responsibility than ever outside the home, we tend to place personal soul-satisfaction at the bottom of our list. Women in the generations before us didn't neglect pivotal female bonding moments, even in the simplest forms: playing cards, going out to brunch, and forming red hat clubs. I want to empower today's women to find new ways to satisfy our friendship needs, alongside the pursuit of achievement in a hyper-tasking, over committed world. Like any accomplishment, personal friendship must be intentional, like the monthly commitment to my dinner club.

Are you intentional about time with your friends? Do you set aside time to nurture meaningful friendships with women? Are you as concerned about your friends' feelings as you are your bosses? As a reliable friend, you are a role model, a cheerleader, and sometimes the stay-up-all-night-and-cry-your-eyes-out partner. Are you willing to model this friendship behavior?

I am so fortunate to have my dinner club friends and my referee friends. They are my sanctuary. They balance me with their opposite lives, amazing talents, adorable children, and special family dramas. My dinner club girls are the only people I have cooked more than 100 meals with, all while talking about our families, friends, and dreams. My dinner club has become a part of my identity, and I do not apologize for this personal time. Are you making time for the girls who balance your life? Are they a "Big Rock" in your weekly calendar?

Stephen R. Covey popularized the illustration of big rocks in the jar. If you aren't familiar, look up the video on YouTube or read it in his book, *First Things First*. The general idea is that in your life you have all kinds of responsibilities and tasks that need to get done each day. Some of them are critical, though not necessarily urgent, and must be completed for you to reach your goals. These are your "big rocks." Big rocks are usually ongoing projects that cannot be rushed or relationships that need long term nurturing. Unfortunately the task of being busy, "little rocks," overrides the mission-critical tasks. You know how your day seemed so busy, yet at the end of it you felt as though nothing was accomplished? That is often because we allow the busy tasks of opening email, answering the phone, or filling out the survey to get in the way of the true big rocks that need undivided attention.

This week:

I will call:

_____

_____

I will enjoy happy hour with:

_____

_____

I will express my appreciation for:

_____

_____

_____

If, like me, you believe one measure of your success on this earth is your relationships with people, then you have to make the people a priority. My girlfriend time is required. Period. And I will schedule it if I am feeling as though I am neglecting those relationships. Below, you can see an example of my weekly planning to include my relationships as big rocks on my weekly to-do list. I write up one of these almost every Sunday night before the week begins.

Big Rocks

1. #SuccessWithoutApology book writing
   a. Edit one chapter (2 hours)
   b. Submit cover to publisher

2. Wystle
   a. Socialize new inventory
   b. Create a special for the week
3. Salon
   a. Promote open chair
   b. Collect rent
   c. Socialize new management
4. Friendships
   a. Beverly – check on Taylor
   b. Meredith – ask about recitals
   c. Dinner club – thank Angie
5. Family
   a. One quiet dinner with husband
   b. Call Sister
   c. Check on Mom's garage project
   d. Text niece about school

If you're losing touch with your girlfriends, it is time to schedule specific friendship-building activities in your calendar. Replace the words "Big Rocks" with "Relationships" and establish set-in-stone tasks to show your friends or family how much you care about and value your connection with them. Reconnect with people who bless you and contribute to your success. Allow them to join the roller coaster of highs and lows with you. #RightNow

Do not apologize for loyalty to your friends. When they are in need, help them. When they hurt, cry with them. When you hurt, anticipate their empathy. When you succeed, receive their compliments. If you don't have great friends, start a dinner club. #ItWorkedForMe

My dinner club girlfriend once made us tank tops for a girls' trip and it said, "If you have friends like mine, raise your glass. If you don't, raise your standards."

My wish to you is that your friends will raise their glass because they have such a great friend like you in their life. And here is a toast to all my friends – I couldn't possibly name them all – but they know who they are and how much I love them. #Cheers

Relationship:

_____

Goal/Task:

_____

Relationship:

_____

Goal/Task:

_____

Relationship:

_____

Goal/Task:

_____

We need women at all levels, including the top, to change the dynamic, reshape the conversation, and make sure women's voices are heard and heeded, not overlooked and ignored.

—Sheryl Sandberg

Chapter Eight
SUPPORTING
OTHER WOMEN

1. Do not apologize for wanting success (being focused and driven).
2 Do not apologize for your motherhood status.
3. Do not apologize for working late.
4. Do not apologize when you pivot.
5. Do not apologize for taking care of yourself.
6. Do not apologize for emotions (yours or others).
7. Do not apologize for friendships and loyalty.

Eighth Commandment: Do not apologize for supporting other women.

9. Do not apologize for being the boss.
10. Do not apologize for reaping the rewards of success.

Sitting on the hillside at recess, we would band together to determine which boy was the cutest, whose house we would stay the night on Friday, and what we would wear to the basketball game. We were a clique. We were *the* clique (in our minds, of course). If you were the boy who broke my friend's heart, you were officially off limits and dead to us all. Did anyone else have this group of girlfriends as a child? Each group may have had their own interests, but all the girls had a group. Maybe you were part of the art group, band group, preppy group, mean-girl group, or athletic group, but more than likely in early elementary school you were part of a group.

As we age, somewhere along the line, society taught girls to climb over one another on the success ladder, rather than pull each other up the rungs. I am not sure when this changed, but it has been detrimental to our collective success. We need to consciously choose to support other women and have each other's backs, just like in grade school. If our girlfriend is sad, we should cry with her. If she is having a terrible day, we should stop and hear her story. And if her husband cheats on her, we should ask her the same question Shari asked me when I showed up heartbroken, drunk, and in tears: "What kind of friend do you want me to be? Am I the friend who tells you everything will be all right or the one who helps you bury his body?" #BestQuestionEver #ExactlyWhatIneeded

This support needs to extend beyond our personal friendships. We need to find ways to support each other in the workplace, whether that is inside or outside the home. When you look at your work environment, is it affirming women's success?

Are you personally fostering women's success? When I asked my friend Teresa how she thought she had best fostered women's success in her companies, she said the most powerful way to support women's success is to demonstrate it. When I pushed her further on the topic, she explained how women need to see other women unapologetically living a life of success. Encourage women to own their role with confidence and happiness as an example to other women who may desire the same role someday.

Women are sometimes antagonistic without intending to be. We have succumbed to cultural stereotypes, and sometimes we don't even recognize our harmful words. Are you unreasonably critical of other women? I admit, I was once more deprecating of women without realizing it. Not because I wanted to be, but because I was unconsciously adopting the ideals and stereotypes of those around me. Guess who was around me in the boardroom, on the court, and at the gym? Men, mostly all men. I noticed I was judging other women as the men judged them. Though I didn't think I was like the men in the room, I too, was criticizing women unfairly.

I challenge you to note the critical words you hear used to describe the women in your workplace Decide if you are judging them differently from your male peers. Are you isolating them, comparing them only to other women? Are you encouraging women to apply for promotions within the company? Does your company have any women in C-level roles? Are females and males awarded the same?

Anyone in sales knows that the last day of the month comes with either great reward or tremendous fear. On one particular month, our New York team hit our sales number - time to celebrate. In our company, sales rewards were paid out in the form of alcohol and bar food. The boss rented a small bar space in New York City and paid for everyone to drink and eat until they needed an Uber ride home. It was the culture. The boys had perfected the ritual. Unfortunately, the five women now on the sales force didn't feel rewarded. We abhorred the two alcohol-ridden hours where men in leadership were able to say whatever they wanted to us, then apologize the day after with "Maybe we should not discuss work when I have had so much to drink." #TrueStory #ActuallyHappened

Women are rarely respected when they go out with the guys, even if they can hang as well as the men. I learned this early in my officiating career, and it proved true in the New York City advertising industry too. So, in this company, where the rituals and rewards were so geared to the men, women were being unfairly penalized both for their participation and their shunning. It was a no-win situation for the women. During this particular company's shift in ownership, I had been retained for my industry relationships, intense understanding of the landscape, and experience forecasting and exceeding sales numbers year after year. Great market credentials and reputation aside, I was never going to break into the "boys' club" in this new company. Not only would I not be invited, but neither would any other females— ever. #StillNoWomenAfter3Years

Though the parent company recruited me and sought my insight during the closing, the leadership of the company refused to allow me into the board meetings once I was in house. It should not have been a surprise when the top brass held the executive retreat one night before the company-wide retreat, inviting every C-level executive except me. Hmmm. #NoGirlsAllowedMontauk

When I subtly mentioned the absence of women on the speakers' panel, in the boardroom, and at the mid-management level, the principal owner did not appreciate my observation. He could have reacted positively to my remark, but instead he defensively responded with a classic "there just are not any qualified women in technology." The response repulsed me. I know that women are graduating with more degrees than men and entering the workforce faster than ever, and so this utterly transparent chauvinism sickened me! Reflecting on the conversation at the round table, he could have responded dozens of ways to give me confidence in his desire to diversify the corporate landscape. Instead he extinguished any hope for female leadership in the company. Have you ever been in this position? Have you ever been influential in an organization that simply didn't want women to be included in the men's club? How did you handle it? Would you handle it differently now? #WomenAreInTechnology #CallingBullShit

Can you be someone's voice today?

How?
_____
_____

What will it potentially cost you?
_____
_____

Is it worth it?
_____
_____

Has anyone ever stood up for you? How?
_____
_____

I left the retreat compelled to advocate for the women in the office, from Kim and Victoria to Jessica and Laura. For any woman working her ass off without recognition or appreciation, I would find ways to elevate her status in the company. During the next six months, even if it would cost me my job, I specifically recognized women's accomplishments in the staff meetings. I nominated them for more responsibility. I defended them when the men spoke condescendingly to them. I privately rallied for their titles and pay to match their increased levels of responsibility. I also encouraged them daily to be their best, regardless of whether they thought anyone noticed. Women in the company were young, talented, and hardworking, but they were not being promoted, paid, or recognized as their male counterparts were. The vice president once called them emotional, difficult, or too flirty to have productive conversations. I was outraged.

Although it might ultimately cost me a promotion or my long-term career with the company, I would push for the praise and recognition of the firm's women. I don't apologize for being their voice, even if it ultimately was at my expense. #MLStillDoesntPromoteFemales #WithoutApology

Maybe you don't want to get fired trying to promote other women, but you do want to make a difference and help young women navigate success. I want to give you specific examples of ways you can support and promote other women in order to help them achieve their highest level of success. While there are other ways, here are a few you can do, specifically if you have a leadership or management role within the company.

1. Recruit and interview more women.
2. Evaluate company policies, parties, and rewards.
3. Celebrate accomplishments of women publicly.
4. Avoid stereotyping women.
5. Mentor girls and women.

Recruitment

First of all, you have to be willing to go out there and actively seek women to apply and interview with your company. In a small company, you have more control over recruitment and retention policies. If you are in a large corporation, you may need to speak with the Human Resources department about ways to attract more women, unless of course there are just no women in your field. #InsertSarcasmHere. Also, there may be women in the company you are overlooking simply because they are not asking for a promotion. I have read multiple articles that say over and over, a man will confidently ask for a promotion before he is qualified, but a woman waits until she is overqualified before even asking. As one *Forbes* article put it, "Men are confident about their ability at 60%, but women don't feel confident until they've checked off each item on the list." [11]

You have most likely heard some version of this comment in your employment career:

> We have seven great candidates for two positions. We have five men and two women. Of the two women, Jane is a better candidate, don't you think?

What happens in the pool of five candidates is the two women end up being singled out against one another. While you may think this increases the odds for the woman (1:2 versus 1:5), it actually doesn't because suddenly the females are isolated into a subcategory. The candidates are not viewed equally. As managers, it is important that we intentionally change this common conversation in the hiring process and evaluate women equally, not just in competition with the people of the same gender.

Evaluate Policy

In my career, I have broken a few glass ceilings and been the only female in the boardroom, on the road, at the golf outing, at the bar—you get the picture. I learned very young to take the jokes, be one of the guys, and hold my own. Then I met Teresa, and I saw a woman in charge doing it differently. Teresa was one of the rising stars in the accounting technology field, and she was awesome. When we met, she was on her way up in a very male-dominated profession, yet she was not trying to be one of the guys. She may have been one of my first true corporate female role models. #SorryINeverToldYouTMac

Teresa simply outworked the boys. She also out-"niced" them. And when she reached the very top, becoming president, she set new rules that were noticeably more inclusive for women in her industry. She guided the change of environment in her organization. Deals were no longer done at the bar closing time. Professionalism in the boardroom meant more than one's mastery of the bar scene.

Celebrate Accomplishments

You may recall in the introductory chapter, I described how differently a male and female respond to accolades for their accomplishments. The woman almost *always* responds with "thank you" and then credits everyone else on the team. A man will feel much more comfortable accepting the credit alone.

If we want our organization or company to recognize women for their accomplishments, strength, vision, and leadership, we must celebrate them and give women the confidence and the okay to accept the credit they have earned. Be clear, I am not bashing men; nor am I saying they need to share the credit. I am saying, in this case, women should take a lesson and just say thank you and quit sharing the responsibility for their success. The next time you close a big sale, write a great report, or finish a project, be prepared to accept the honors that come with it.

Stereotyping

Women can be moody.

Women can be emotional.

Women can be bossy.

Women can be selfish.

Women can be self-absorbed.

Women can use their looks to their advantage.

Every description above has been used to negatively stereotype women. For some reason, these same descriptions are never used to discredit men. But did you know?

Men can be moody.

Men can be emotional.

Men can be bossy.

Men can be selfish.

Men can be self-absorbed.

Men can use their looks to their advantage.

These descriptions have subliminally slipped into our vocabulary, and we don't realize that we use these preconceived notions to hurt our very own women peeps. When the VP told me Kim was too emotional, I quickly responded with "She is not nearly as emotional as James or Rob or Scott. Those three guys are the most emotional people in the company." Of course, he had never considered those guys emotional, only driven and passionate. That was the last time he called Kim emotional, at least to me. I refused to allow him to stereotype her simply because she was a female. Where can you make a difference in your company culture? Where can you stop the stereotypes that plague our gender? #JamesWillreadThisAndNotDenyHeIsEmotional

Mentorship

Mentor-schmentor, you may say. I know, I know, everyone is talking about it. But seriously, you must mentor people. You must mentor women. With less than 10 percent of the Fortune 500 companies being led by women, our role models are few and far between. In most professions women are far behind in leadership, and sometimes young girls simply don't have anyone to aspire to be when they grow up. It is incumbent upon you to help the women who come after you, to support the women who rise with you, and to cheer for those who pass you on the way up the ladder. Right now - tell me - who can you mentor?

What female can you mentor personally?

_____

What female can you mentor professionally?

_____

What female can you mentor spiritually?

_____

_____

Make the decision to help other women. You cannot let these statistics continue:

- Only 4.4 percent of Fortune 500 CEOs are female.[2]
- Only 11 percent of Silicon Valley executives are female.[3]
- We are 51 percent of the population.

We _need_ role models at every level so young women entering the field know it is possible. Hopefully we can see this shift positively over the next few years.

After you decide whom you will mentor, make it official. Make a list of what you will do with or for each woman and when you will do it. How will you make a difference in your mentee's vision of what a successful woman can and should be?

What will you offer your mentee(s) this week?

_____

_____

_____

When will you fulfill your mentor duties this week?

_____

_____

_____

You are strong enough, smart enough, and able enough to encourage other women. If you are reading this book, you are already a #girlboss, or you are on your way to becoming one, so I know women would benefit from your expertise and experience. If you are in college, encourage your peers or someone in high school. Encourage your younger sister or niece to be proud of her accomplishments, to be fearless in her dreams, and to quit apologizing for success. If you are the president of your company or the anchor on the morning news, women need to see your successes and failures so they can learn from you. Give back. Be a mentor. Encourage other women to be even more successful than you are today.

Do not apologize for supporting other women. They depend on you.

Because I said so, that's why.

—Mom

Chapter Nine
BEING THE BOSS

1. Do not apologize for wanting success (being focused and driven).
2. Do not apologize for your motherhood status.
3. Do not apologize for working late.
4. Do not apologize when you pivot.
5. Do not apologize for taking care of yourself.
6. Do not apologize for emotions (yours or others).
7. Do not apologize for friendships and loyalty.
8. Do not apologize for supporting other women.

Ninth Commandment: Don't apologize for being the boss.

10. Do not apologize for reaping the rewards of success.

"Why do I have to do the dishes?" says every child. "Because I said so," responds every mom in the world. You remember, your parents said it more times that you can count. If you are a parent, you probably say it now too. When my mom said, "Because I said so," our debate was finished. Mom had given the final word, and she made no apologies for being the boss of our life. As you have learned, I didn't birth and raise any children, but I do have several employees and subcontractors who occasionally have to hear, "Because I said so, that's why." #GirlBoss

We can all empathize with the employees' pain at times. I work to understand their veiwpoints and concerns before making a final decision. But truly, no one fears failure as much as the boss or owner. In the case of the stylists I described earlier in the book, I knew the loss would hurt me financially, and the salon image would be at risk. Yet, at this critical moment I decided I would not be bullied by fear of loss. So I held my ground. I implemented my vision, and now, a year later, my vision has come true: I have a spa and salon full of people who love to brainstorm new ideas and keep up with the trends. It was scary. It was painful, but it was necessary and right for the good of the whole company. It is how bosses have to think. We have to think beyond our right-now needs and wants to the long-term success for the entire organization.

Whether the CEO of a large corporation, owner of a small salon, or mother of your children, being the boss comes with great authority and responsibility. My girlfriends and I are confident when it comes to running our homes. Rarely do they make apologies for raising children their own way or for the rules they set for them, even if it looks different from their best friend's. Neither my friends nor I make apologies for how we like our laundry folded, our dishes set in the dishwasher (forks pointing up in my house), or our beds to be made, but we are caught sometimes apologizing for demanding the best from our peers and subordinates at work. I want to encourage women to take some of those mom skills and use them in the office (similar message to earlier chapters). Occasionally, you can even use the phrase "because I said so." #MomBossWithoutApology

Some of us significantly downplay our leadership role and executive status when we are among our peers or friends. I have a girlfriend who tells me she rarely admits she has a PhD because people (and by people, she means women peers) treat her like she is suddenly better than them or a hoity-toity know-it-all. Do you unconsciously and unnecessarily downplay your personal success or accomplishments? Do you apologize for being in charge at work? Why do you not own your boss role at work like you do at home? There are two reasons I used to apologize; maybe they are the reasons you apologize too.

1. I feared being labeled bossy or bitchy.
2. I feared outshining the men in my life.

Remember my mom's gymnastics business? At fourteen years old, I had my first paid job working for her. I was my mom's assistant teacher, spotting back handsprings, leading stretches and exercises, and demonstrating the tricks. Each day after school you could hear me say, "Point your toes, straighten your legs, tuck your chin, ta-da!" I was a good gymnast (not Olympic material, remember), but I was an even better "bossypants."

I am not ashamed to say I earned the "bossy" title at a young age. I say I earned it because, quite frankly, I *was* acting immature and bossy. But I was learning. My mom was mentoring me and showing me an example of the kind boss who took every detail seriously. I am somewhat embarrassed by how long it took me to understand the difference between being the boss and being bossy. I still check myself every now and then when I realize I am barking orders, rather than guiding and directing. Thanks, Tina Fey, for writing *Bossypants* (#BossyPants) to help us understand it is a normal part of our leadership growth.

My friend Linque and I were youth co-directors at a church while attending college. After three years together, he gave me one of my greatest #GirlBoss compliments. He said, "Rachael has a way of getting you to do things that you never even knew you volunteered to do, until after you have completed the project and are proud of yourself.

Then you realize she actually put you up to it. She is the master delegator." I loved this compliment and still believe delegation is one of my greatest gifts, nearly twenty years later. I can keep many people busy at the same time, working toward a single goal. Unfortunately, the stereotype for women who delegate, give directions, or lead has been that she must be bossy or bitchy. Thank God, the stereotype is changing and improving; thank you to all the #girlboss women before me who've paved the way. It is our responsibility to *not* perpetuate this label. We need to be overly careful when we judge women in charge. Do not call them bitchy, even if they may be, because that label and stereotype ends up hurting us all. #ProudBoss #MasterDelegator #BossNotBossy

I am so thankful for the women before me who have helped squash the stereotype that women need to be hard-shelled and calloused to be respected as the boss. It is becoming more acceptable for woman to lead, like my friend Teresa, with kindness, likeability, and intelligence. I no longer fear being called bossy because I know the people who say that are intimidated by my leadership. I do not fear or shy away from their label because it is usually more of a reflection of their close-mindedness about women's success than it is a true depiction of me. If you would like to see a great commercial reflecting the difference between how we label men versus women, you should check out a great Pantene ad I came across. You can find it by searching, "Labels Against Women— Pantene." It is a great depiction, unfortunately, of how we mislabel women who are demonstrating the exact same boss actions as men.

The other reason I believe women apologize is the desire to not outshine their husbands or partners. I was married to my first husband for ten years, and when we first married, he made more money than I did. I was much younger than him and that seemed "normal," but then, as my career advanced, I began to make more money than he did. Yet it was really important to me that he appeared to be the breadwinner. I am not sure where that originated or why I wanted him to look like the moneymaker, but I did. And I did a great deal of hiding my personal success and downplaying my goals, aspirations, and achievements in order to uphold this image.

As I observe women around me, I see signs of this in other couples too. I, for one, love men, and I love my man in particular. It is important to me to make him feel masculine, in-charge, macho and important. But what I've learned over the years is that his significance doesn't have to be at the expense of mine. I don't have to apologize for my success to foster and support his. One valuable lesson I have learned in my second marriage is that my success can be celebrated without fear of taking my husband's "man card." He is macho and significant even if my paycheck is more each month. He doesn't find me bossy; he finds me sexy and talented as the boss. And I thank God each day for that. He has never asked me to apologize for being the boss at home or at work. #GodBlessedMeWithAGreatMan #IDidBetterRound2

My earlier salon episode is an example of where being the boss is not easy. In this case, it probably didn't matter if I were a man or a woman delivering the news because I don't believe it was a gender issue; it was a "being the boss" issue. Making difficult decisions, being a leader, trying to predict the benefits and consequences, and then moving forward and upward with the business is part of being the boss. In the companies I own, I am the boss unapologetically because it is my livelihood. Sometimes I work for other people, and their expectation is for me to carry out the role as though I own the company. Either way, someone is depending on me making the best judgement decisions possible. I can confidently tell you, sometimes I am overwhelmed and sometimes I feel only 60% qualified (remember how men will statistically go for it when they feel at least 60% capable). But rest assured, I no longer apologize, I simply do my best and go forward armed with the best research, knowledge, and advisor group possible. Despite my early career perceptions, I am not meant to be only the second person in charge—in title, in pay, or in responsibility. I am born to be the leader.
#LeadersDoMakeMistakes #IAmNotWithoutFault

As the boss of your life or your business, you make tough decisions, and most of the time you need to so without apology. Here are eight skills for being the boss, at home or in the workplace, that I believe we can all continue to sharpen. I still sometimes apologize for these,

#DamnIt, but I know if I want us to be solid, successful #GirlBosses, we need to sharpen our skills and our confidence to carry them out:

1. Setting deadlines

2. Gathering consensus

3. Committing a personal leadership style

4. Focusing

5. Saying no

6. Pivoting

7. Failing up

8. Setting boundaries

Critical company decisions are rarely made by committee, and the toughest decisions of all will usually make someone unhappy. One tough decision for me is to tell people they cannot be present at important life events. I want my peers and employees to be able to attend their child's recital, or take that trip, or go to that conference, but sometimes I have to say *no*. What if I tell one person yes because I know she won't leave without completing every task on her plate, yet I tell another person no because I am not confident she will fulfill her duties unless she is on task in the office? It is tough. A former Dallas Cowboys coach was once quoted as saying he treated every player differently to treat them the same. He understood that every player didn't react or respond to the exact same punishment or treatment. You understand this if you have siblings or children. One child fears a spanking, and another fears the look of disappointment. So to treat each of them the same, you punish them differently. This is a magnificent leadership style and truly difficult to emulate. I strive to treat each of my employees differently, yet model principles in each style so they can anticipate my reaction.

These eight skills are further broken down on my blog and they are key to becoming an unapologetic #GirlBoss. Be sure to check them out at RachaelMelot.com

I continue to take my own advice and work to improve my behavior daily. My challenge is for you to recognize the apology addiction and refrain from making the same mistakes I made. Stop apologizing; instead, pursue and accept the titles and opportunities you deserve and want.

Do you want to be the boss one day? It is okay to do it your way. Do you want to earn more? Know your worth and don't undervalue yourself. Do you want to publish a book or launch a small business? Go ahead and write the business plan today. You need to stop apologizing for working to make dreams come true for yourself. Stop apologizing for making sacrifices in the short term for your long-term happiness and fulfillment. Stop sabotaging your success in order to please others. Be empowered, knowing you can do it just a little differently from society or from what your network expects you to do. You can start today. Go ahead; do it.

Because I am the boss—and I said so. ☺

*You don't have to flaunt your success,
but you don't have to apologize for it either.*

—Gene Stallings

Chapter Ten
REWARDS OF SUCCESS

1. Do not apologize for wanting success (being focused and driven).
2. Do not apologize for your motherhood status.
3. Do not apologize for working late.
4. Do not apologize when you pivot.
5. Do not apologize for taking care of yourself.
6. Do not apologize for emotions (yours or others).
7. Do not apologize for friendships and loyalty.
8. Do not apologize for supporting other women.
9. Do not apologize for being the boss.

Tenth Commandment: Do not apologize for your rewards of success.

On a cold, dreary day in early April, I roll out of bed, put on a ball cap, and head to the nail salon. No different from any other nail appointment, except the new bags I am carrying under my eyes are a result of crying myself to sleep at night. My new normal: pretend to be fine all day, climb into my bed alone, and cry until I fall asleep. Two months after the divorce, this is still my routine most nights I am home. In an effort to appear as though I have my life together, and as a way of doing something to help me feel good about myself, I always keep my nail appointment! I may miss the dentist, hair, or gynecologist appointment, but girl never miss her nail appointment! Girl cannot function without her nails looking beautifully manicured. #CountryGirlWithCityGirlNails

For anyone else who is a regular at the nail salon, you know the five minutes when you are trapped under the blue lamp waiting for your polish to dry, when it seems like the longest eight minutes in history? I dread those painful, still minutes. On this particular morning, the time almost got the best of me. A woman, who I would most likely call an acquaintance, kindly says hello and sits near me. She expresses sorrow for my divorce and my ex-husband's actions. I graciously thank her. Then it comes. She asks the question—the question *everyone* seems to be asking me these days:

"Are you going to keep your house?"

"Yes," I respond matter-of-factly, hoping this to-the-point answer ends the inquisition. But no, somehow it never does. The seemingly obligatory next statement is "Really, why? It's such a big house."

Yes, I know the home is big. Yes, I know it is a lot of house for just one person. I know. As a matter of fact, I know everything there is to know about the house. I drew the plans, designed every cabinet and cubbyhole, personally dug the footing with a shovel, and have lived in it for nine years—I know exactly how big the house is. I know what it costs. I also know you never would have asked a man this question if he kept the house post divorce.

So my answer is always the same: "Yes, I know it's a big house, but it is mine and I paid for it. So I am keeping it." Should be the end of the conversation, right? Generally though, it's not.

I can't explain how sick I was of hearing the questions about the house. Never mind my emotional state—people were much more consumed with the pending state of my property. Seriously! Would it make them feel better if I moved into a smaller house? I hated it at the time, but I can see how this house became the benchmark against which people gauged my post-divorce status. I was just going to have to learn to accept this new identity in my small town. People's perceptions are funny, but the reality is that because I kept the house, the bankers are so much more curious to what I do for a living. The lenders seem to think I am a brilliant businesswoman. Now they want to take me to play golf.
#IwasTheMemberAllAlong #StillSameWoman
#HowDoYouLikeMeNow

I didn't keep the house for status or recognition, but in retrospect, I believe keeping my home impacted my local reputation much more than I had anticipated. But now I realize keeping the house became a symbol of my survival. I had won; my ex-husband had not. I was able to live in and maintain the house without a husband upon whom to rely. This gave me an unexpected sense of confidence, of strength, after I had been emotionally beat up by my tragic life events. I would not apologize for keeping my house. I had done this; I had attained the success and income to do this on my own. People would just have to accept that. #InterestingSociety #WomanInTheBackground

I—the woman of the household; the secret family breadwinner; the newly single, unpretentious, scared to death woman—was keeping the big house on the golf course, come hell or high water! I was determined to find a way, and no one could make me apologize for keeping what I had earned, even if it looked nontraditional or unconventional in small-town Midwest America.

Interestingly enough, I had grown up with a vision much like many women in the Midwest, or more specifically the region referred to as the Bible Belt, that the husband was to be the "man of the house," spiritually and financially. And I had been content, in our ten years of marriage, positioning him as the financial leader of our home, even after the earnings changed and I was the one paying all the bills with my income. While the responsibility for our living expenses shifted largely onto me, the public perception of our finances and consequent obligations did not change, and I was okay with that while I was married.

Post divorce, the secret was out. Without the shield of a presumptive man of the house, it was all me. People would see; they would undeniably have assumptions about my net worth and earning capabilities. Honestly, I was scared to death. But I was determined to keep the house and maintain my lifestyle—regardless of what the naysayers thought. I built a budget and set aside money to pay people to do the things my ex-husband had previously done. First and foremost was a great yard guy (because heaven knows I have no interest in the actual grass). But remember, people's perceptions are their reality, and regardless of how broken and disheveled I was on the inside, I was not going to let my yard reveal my emotional trauma.

So I budgeted, I pruned, I pulled weeds, I fertilized, and I planted. I hid my insecurities. And when my neighbors drove by and I was pruning trees at six o'clock on a Saturday morning, I was disguising my sadness with what looked like pride and hard work.

Thus, I finish this book with this as my final chapter. The tenth commandment of #SuccessWithoutApology is to not apologize for the fruits of your labor, literally and figurately speaking. Women are so guilty of downplaying those hard-earned material items. For example, the last time someone complimented your shoes, how did you respond? More often than not, the everyday woman responds with something like "Oh thanks, I got them on sale last year" or "Thank you, I found them online for much less than retail price." Rather than the sufficient "thank you," we explain how we got a deal, or that our spouse bought it for us, or basically any other way of saying we are too ashamed to have spent our hard-earned money on the item. We kind of, well, apologize.

On the cover of this book, I debated for weeks whether or not to include my convertible car in the image background. I received feedback from several women who felt you may not read my book because the car may give the appearance of a braggart, or someone too arrogant or unrelatable. I recognize everyone's idea of success is not owning a Mercedes Benz, but after contemplating their feedback, I decided that not placing the car on the cover was actually giving in to my own insecurities around earning power. I earned that car. I worked my butt off for that vehicle, and I am proud to have been able to purchase it on my own. Honestly, cars are the very last thing in the world that "impress" me, but I have wanted a convertible my whole life, and I am at a stage of life where it isn't too impractical. So I bought one. I placed this car on the cover because I want you to know that if you work hard and choose to spend your money on a new car, new boobs, an oversized mansion, or a vacation, it is okay! You don't have to apologize for what you can afford. #YourMoneyYourDecision

Funny story though, I traded in my ten-year-old truck with two hundred thousand miles on it to buy this little eight-year-old hot-rod convertible for cash. (See how I just downplayed the car purchase so you didn't think negatively of me?) See we all do it. *Stop it.* I don't want to apologize for driving a cute little convertible. It is one of the luxuries of working so very hard each day. I will no longer apologize for my successes.

One of my stylists, whom I really admire, gave me a book to read by Dr. Wayne W. Dyer. In the book, *Excuses Be Gone*, he asks the reader, "What am I unwilling to think or do, in order to become all that I am destined to become?" This resonated with me in so many ways, and as I made the decision to leave the little red car on the cover, I am confident that my readers are willing to think and do, unlike others, so they can pursue their passions. Maybe your proudest accomplishment or reward is a child graduating with an accounting degree, a pair of red heels, or a monthlong mission trip to Africa. Maybe you earned a top corner office or a Mercedes Benz. My advice to you is not to flaunt your rewards or successes but not to be ashamed of them either. When I see a woman with a great watch, handbag, or pair of heels, I compliment her and expect her to say only thank you. I want you to live within your means, and I want you to spoil yourself with the luxuries you have earned. Most importantly, I want you to do so without apology. It is time to stop apologizing for what you have earned through hard work, determination, and focus.

Do you have something in your life that you have earned but always apologize for or make excuses for when complimented? Why do you make the apology? What insecurity are you hiding?

Are you ashamed (kinda) of something you have earned?

_____

_____

Why? Why do you apologize for it?

_____

_____

As you finish *The Ten Commandments of #SuccessWithoutApology*, I suggest you stop apologizing. Stop other women from apologizing unnecesarily and let our thank you's be enough. Your words are mission critical to people's perception of you. Two actions to take note of and begin to correct today:

1. Stop your thank you, with thank you.
2. Stop accepting other women's apologies. Ask her to simply receive the compliment with a thank you.

IN CONCLUSION

May it be motivation for you that I am not an independently wealthy, multimillionaire, trust-fund child. I am not the CEO of a Fortune 500 company. I am not Sheryl Sandberg or Ivanka Trump, women who have "made it." I am simply a disciplined, hardworking, God-fearing daughter of a cowboy and a travel agent. I am the woman next door who owns a small business. I am an entrepreneur who stayed at my salon until 1:30 a.m. painting the room for a new stylist because that was the only time that worked for the business. I am you, or who you may be one day, or who you once were in your lifetime. I understand you.

I come from humble beginnings on a cattle ranch in Oklahoma, and I work diligently to thrive in a society that encourages women's rights yet still underpays me, undervalues me, and labels me bossy just because I am a girl. I am not apologizing for being a woman, and I don't want any pity. But rest assured, I am not content with the world I live in today. I am working hard to adjust the mind-set about women like me and you. I hope this book has encouraged and inspired you to unapologetically be the boss of your life. You can be the boss of your finances, your faith, and your family, if you want to be. You no longer need to apologize for your dreams and desires. Go back to the introductory chapter where you wrote your objectives for reading this book. Did you gain what you had hoped? Are you motivated to build a career, family, and legacy on your terms? Do you want to change the world's view of successful women?

In true random Rachael fashion, I would like to close this book with a quote from one woman who refuses to apologize for her success, her way: Lady Gaga.

> *I used to walk down the street like I was a superstar... I want people to walk around delusional about how great they can be—and then to fight so hard for it every day that the lie becomes the truth.*

—Lady Gaga

Go ahead, dream your delusional dream of grandeur and success. Then fight like hell until that fantasy becomes your reality. And as you reach your goals, own the rewards. #SuccessWithoutApology

ACKNOWLEDGMENTS

There are a few people I want to recognize for their support in my writing this book:

- The women of the George W. Bush Women in Fellowship class of 2015–16 who nudged me to write this book, *thank you*. The year I spent with each of you, especially my friend and mentee Hanen, truly changed my life and my perspective on my role in changing the world's perception of women and our success.

- Mom, my greatest inspiration and teacher of success, clothed in grace and compassion.

- Jason Melot, the love of my life and my perfect partner - thank you for enduring the year of writing (and all the stress that accompanied it).

- To my dinner club girls, who have shared this road with me for the past ten years. They have loved me, forgiven me, carried me, and inspired me, and I love them all with my whole heart!

- Madison Taylor for taking the photos for the cover of the book – I look forward to watching your growth and #SuccessWithoutApology.

- Lastly – to every person who read and revised my writing over the last 12 months. I couldn't have done it without you

REFERENCES

[1] Drexler, P. (2013, August 23). Why You Need To Brag More (And How To Do It). Retrieved May 7, 2017, from https://www.forbes.com/sites/peggydrexler/2013/08/23/why-you-need-to-brag-more-and-how-to-do-it/

[2] USUAL WEEKLY EARNINGS OF WAGE AND SALARY WORKERS—FIRST ... (n.d.). Retrieved May 7, 2017, from https://www.bing.com/cr?IG=8D2D36398B15 4A2F9BBC22029329EB51&CID=3F6DF6FF351B62100697FC6D341D632A&rd =1&h=drrMpnZUh3zw6IeSmuaMDRxBrHTEFO5crokKSTXypgo&v=1&r=https %3a%2f%2fwww.bls.gov%2fnews.release%2fpdf%2fwkyeng.pdf&p=DevEx,5060.1

[3] Chua-Eoan, H., & Dias, E. (2013, December 11). Pope Francis, The People's Pope. Retrieved May 7, 2017, from http://poy.time.com/2013/12/11/person-of-the-year-pope-francis-the-peoples-pope/

[4] Kirchgaessner, S. (2015, February 11). Pope Francis: not having children is selfish. Retrieved May 7, 2017, from https://www.theguardian.com/world/2015/feb/11/pope-francis-the-choice-to-not-have-children-is-selfish

[5] Remaining childless – selfish or noble? (n.d.). Retrieved May 9, 2017, from http://www.wnd.com/2015/07/remaining-childless-selfish-or-noble/

[6] "Workplace Health Promotion." *Centers for Disease Control and Prevention.* Centers for Disease Control and Prevention, 01 Apr. 2016. Web. 9 May 2017.

[7] "14 Surprising Causes of Dehydration." *Health.com.* N.p., n.d. Web. 9 May 2017.

[8] "Exercise Habits of Ultra-Successful People." *Andrew Merle.* N.p., n.d. Web. 9 May 2017.

[9] Merle, Andrew. "The Reading Habits of Ultra-Successful People." *Observer*. N.p., 21 Apr. 2016. Web. 11 May 2017.

[10] Corley, Thomas C. *Rich Habits: the Daily Success Habits of Wealthy Individuals*. N.p.: Itasca , 2010. Print.

[11] Nancy F. Clark, "Act Now to Shrink the Confidence Gap," WomensMedia,